God Loves Messy People

*For Gill
with love*

Bonnie Keen

*Bonnie
Psalms 34:18*

HARVEST HOUSE™ PUBLISHERS
EUGENE, OREGON

Cover by Left Coast Design, Portland, Oregon

GOD LOVES MESSY PEOPLE
Copyright © 2002 by Bonnie Keen
Published by Harvest House Publishers
Eugene, Oregon 97402

Library of Congress Cataloging-in-Publication Data
Keen, Bonnie, 1955–
   God loves messy people / Bonnie Keen.
     p. cm.
     ISBN 0-7369-1012-3
     1. Women—Religious life. 2. Christian life—Meditations. I. Title.
   BV4527 .K442 2002
   248.4—dc21   2002017266

Printed in the United States of America

02 03 04 05 06 07 08 09 10 / BP-CF / 10 9 8 7 6 5 4 3 2 1

To all the messy, beloved ones of Jesus.
May we embrace the humanity of His companionship
and find ourselves transformed into messengers of His hope.

Praise for the Book *God Loves Messy People*

"I admire Bonnie so much....I love that she is speaking so honestly about things that many in the church are afraid to touch...the messiness of our lives this side of heaven. Not only would I call Bonnie a friend—I would call her one of my heroes in the faith!"

—**Kim Hill**, recording artist and worship leader

"With the sweet aroma of God's grace leaking out all over the place from the broken places of her own messy heart, Bonnie invites us to see how wondrously consistent God has been throughout the history of redemption. He loves messy people—always has, always will.

"With the insight of a fellow pilgrim, Bonnie tells the stories of friends in life and friends in Scripture who are ongoing targets and recipients of God's outrageous love—because of their messes, not because of their promise. In fact, Bonnie helps us to see and enjoy that we are a chosen people, not a choice people! This is good news, indeed!"

—**Scotty Smith**, author of *Objects of His Affection: Coming Alive to the Compelling Love of God* and Senior Pastor of Christ Community Church, Franklin, Tennessee

"When I go to read something Bonnie has written, I know I am going to be blessed because she speaks of her own struggles with such honesty and transparency that I am moved to want to do the same. Honesty is the first step towards truth...and truth sets us free.

"I also love her latest work because of the deep realization I came away with—that God loves me more than I ever give Him credit for...that He loves me in spite of the messes I can make with my life...and that He never abandons me. This book makes me want to know Jesus and follow after Him all the more. Bonnie Keen is one of my heroes!

—**Dennis Jernigan**, Here To Him Music recording artist, worship leader, and author of *This Is My Destiny: Finding Your Identity in Christ*

CONTENTS

THE PHOTOS IN GOD'S WALLET

I am in love with how God loves our messy world. In all our sloppy journeys, soul-worn seasons, good intentions gone belly-up, in all our stubborn tenacity to find the gold at the end of the rainbow, we are, every one of us, at some point, just messy people. You can dress us up and parade us around, but hidden under our well-coifed exteriors often lies a soul in disarray. Yet we are loved. Loved in spite of our messy lives. Loved in the midst of them. Loved through the very places that cannot be explained away. The places that are simply messy.

Messy or not, it matters little to God. He's like a proud father who can't help but pull out the photos in his wallet and brag on his children. We are the faces in His family album. Our names are written on His hand. There is a page for each of us in God's family scrapbook, and He adores us. We are His creation—His idea—and He never gives up on any of us. Not one messy creature.

Wrapping our minds around such a concept is a real twister. For God not only loves the lovable, His face also brightens up when He thinks of the underdogs, the unlikely ones, and those the world declares losers. Heaven rejoices over each messy, beloved person as gleefully as it does over hundreds of the other, less-tattered of earth's children. We all matter, infinitely and forever, to our Creator. He wants us to know Him, to know His love and acceptance.

Yet, through the maze of our needing to be accepted and feeling unworthy because of what life throws our way and what we blunder into, it is nearly impossible for us to believe that a heavenly Creator, perfect in every way, could love us. The snares set out to trip up us humans are innumerable and wildly varied in their seduction and devastation. At some crossroads, at some windfall of circumstance, all of us, if we are honest, will feel unworthy of love, rejected by God, forsaken, alone—in many cases—as if we've run out of time.

Clee

A WARNING ABOUT THE MESSY PART of living should come with our birth certificates.

> *"Welcome to the world. Your life will be a spectacular, breathtaking adventure. At times, you will be speechless in the presence of the beauty and joy you will experience. Other times the wind will be knocked out of you. The rug will be pulled out from under you. Don't forget to read the fine print! There you'll find the words no one wants to read. Disappointment, doubts, and heartache are all included."*

Why is it that we are taken by surprise by the ugly underbelly of life? Why do we expect the best from a world steeped in pain? Continually we find ourselves blindsided by reality. Every new morning offers another chance to admit our inadequacy—once again for this new day, a chance to accept the bewildering ecstasy of God's grace. Why is it so difficult to accept such a love when His grace is the one gift that can penetrate the messy corners of our worlds?

Life, as Henri Nouwen so eloquently wrote, is a kiss where sadness and joy intersect.

> *Our life is a short time in expectation, a time in which sadness and joy kiss each other at every moment...In every satisfaction, there is an awareness of limitations. In every success, there is a fear of jealousy. Behind every smile, there is a tear. In every embrace, there is loneliness. In every friendship, distance...But this intimate experience in which every bit of life is touched by a bit of death can point us beyond the limits of our existence...when our hearts will be filled with perfect joy, a joy that no one can take from us.*

We live, determined to find a steady path while weaving in and out of moments where sadness and joy coexist. Life offers us a pen and blank sheet of paper on which to write our stories. Filling in the blanks with our choices of how to respond to our humanity is up to each of us. All must choose one way or the other how to respond to our messy experiences. Even refusing to respond is in itself a response.

We hit walls and fall down. Bruised and battered, we contemplate tearing down the wall we've bumped up against, or we refuse to come near it again.

Expectations of what life should be, could be, or should have been, what it ought or ought not to look like, are the wild cards in this messy game. For life is utterly unpredictable, which highly frustrates the control we humans want to cling to. There is nothing under the sun that is certain—except that the unexpected will come swooping down on us.

Compounding the obvious uncertainties are the closet disappointments that needle, that pick away at the subconscious. None of us live up to our own expectations. Our humanity breeds in us the seed of unworthiness, urges us into a fierce fight for a presentable sense of self-worth. Yet, when our expectations are dashed, it lays the groundwork for our feeling forsaken, tricked by life or by God or by "fate." Losses and grief lead down the path of loneliness and depression.

But there can be glory as well as agony in the messiness of being a human. Under piles of dashed expectations, sometimes a new dream lies waiting to be explored. Losing can translate into gaining if we allow the losses to nourish the more tender sides of our nature. Out of our firsthand experience, we can give understanding to others who suffer similar losses—thus transforming our pain into a redemptive arena for commiseration and restoration.

Nothing is wasted in our losses if we allow God to use these times to teach us, and those around us, the beauty of being broken in the hands of a loving God. Our losses have the unlikely potential to bring monumental gain.

Clee

THE BIGGEST MISTAKE ANY OF US CAN MAKE is to think that we are alone in our chaotic lives, beyond help. Churches, Bible classes, and the tone of our Western Christian culture have, at times, promoted the spoken and unspoken message that we have to be cleaned up in order to be loved by God. Messy lives are rejected, although there isn't one of us who doesn't have one! We clean up the stories of the men and women of the Bible, emphasizing their heroics and robbing them of their humanity. Many of the biblical characters we tend to think of now as larger than life, suffered the same disillusionment and feeling of unworthiness, the same loneliness and being forsaken by God, as the rest of us.

Job's wife, for example, especially intrigues me. When she and her God-fearing husband lost their entire family and estate, when he suffered from terrible physical illness, she told Job to "curse God and die." Their life wasn't supposed to play out this way! Hadn't she lost her family and suffered along with her husband too? Her responses to their plight weren't so noble. But we aren't always high-minded when at some point faith and life come crashing down around us, bringing unexpected disappointment. It's hard for me to point a finger at Job's wife without having to admit that I relate to her reaction and wonder if I wouldn't have said the same thing...or worse.

The Samaritan woman drifted in and out of marriages and was an outcast in the eyes of the people of her day. Yet Jesus spoke to her at the well, and chose her to be part of a teaching story that we continue to tell today. Moses, not exactly the speaker of the year, reluctantly obeyed God's call to be the spokesman for the Hebrews and lead the Israelites out of their bondage in Egypt. Hannah was accused of being drunk, yet her faithfulness brought her the very thing she longed for most. Martha struggled with "busyness" and forgot to make time to listen. The prodigal son squandered away his inheritance. Zaccheus was despised for his cheating, for his mercenary job as a tax collector. And when things got tough, it was a Roman soldier, despised by the Jewish people, who showed the greatest faith Jesus had seen in His walk on Earth.

David, a man after God's own heart, committed murder and adultery and cried out for forgiveness from a state of deep depression. God's back seemed to be turned to him. He wept for the sweet intimacy of the relationship he had changed by the messiness of his choices. He pleaded with

God like the rest of us do when a black hole of misery threatens to suck us under.

God used all kinds of messy people in their messy conditions and messy lives to carry out His work, His plans, His mercy, and His great acts of redemption. God still uses messy people today in the same way.

Philip Yancey writes in *Soul Survivor* that "saints are 'life-givers,' who make others come alive in a new way, a garden-variety human being through whose life the power and the glory of God are made manifest even though the saint himself may be standing knee-deep in muck."

Clee~

THE STORIES OF PEOPLE IN THIS BOOK point over and over again to how disheveled lives are miraculously swept up by God as He brings order from disorder, hope from despair, and deep trust from shallow waters of doubt. God is in the business of cleaning up this messy world. You'll hear the story of Sandy, who stayed faithful despite her terrible battle with cancer. You'll meet Regina, a prostitute and drug addict, who found that God covers the messiest of lives with His grace. I'll tell you about Parwin, a Muslim by birth, who discovered God in her desperation to stay alive in an abusive marriage. You'll also read about Garry, Tim, Steve, Sue, Mary, Marlei, Patty Sue, Diana, and the lessons that can be learned from each of their lives.

Here is story after story of how life is undeniably unpredictable and challenging, and how the grace of God, as Anne Lamott writes in *Traveling Mercies*, "meets us where we are, but never leaves us where it found us." I pray that these life-giving men and women I describe will spark in you vivid pictures of real people and the way God used their helplessness—pictures that will translate into hope for our own messy lives. These "life-givers" found hope when they were knee-deep in the muck.

When God set our story in motion, it wasn't supposed to be messy. But God isn't afraid of our messes. From the dirt of His creation, He formed His people in His likeness. When sin entered the world and gave birth to its deadly offspring of pride, deceit, selfishness, sexual desecration, murder, jealousy, hatred, and anger, God rolled up His sleeves and fought for His creation. He isn't put off by our blunders, failures, excuses, or fears.

It's as if God said to Himself, "I did not create this world for confusion and pain. Humans were made by My hand, in My own image, to dance and sing and walk with Me. How can I build a bridge for them to cross over to Me? How can I comprehend their predicament?

"I must meet them on their turf.

"I must send a piece of Myself—My heart—I must send My Son to live with them.

"I will learn what it is to be human, and in that process I will give Myself to them to prove My love, My mercy, My grace. This act will carry an eternal guarantee to My messy, precious children that they will never be forsaken and alone.

"Too many pictures in My wallet are missing."

Where Is God?

My friends, do not be surprised at the terrible trouble which now comes to test you. Do not think that something strange is happening to you…After you suffer for a short time, God, who gives all grace, will make everything right. He will make you strong and support you and keep you from falling.

1 PETER 4:12; 5:10

FIRSTHAND RUBBLE

Bonnie's Story

"TERRIBLE TROUBLE" ARRIVES CUSTOM-MADE for each of us. My own season of trouble certainly seemed as terrible as anything I could imagine. Yet, what God allows others to endure makes my story seem like a walk in the park. I have never buried a child, I have never suffered through cancer or watched a loved one die slowly. But all pain is relative—all pain promises suffering.

There was a decade in my life that spanned an especially messy stretch of trouble, trouble that led me through a great testing of my faith. Many times I felt as if I were drowning in the challenges of my circumstances. I was dog-paddling with everything I could muster against a black tide of trouble, which left me exhausted emotionally, physically, and spiritually.

When I finally stopped thrashing in the water, to my surprise I was able to float. My astonished eyes saw scattered glimpses of light penetrating the darkness. Burned into me from my season of terrible trouble was the searing reality of Jesus Christ and His love for me. From this time on, Christ became piercingly alive, human, real—and I came to the truest, most intimate personal experience of the mystery and miracle of His grace.

God promises not to give us more than we can take. However, life piles misery on our heads until it feels like every last breath of our faith will be choked off. God is ever-present and faithful even in the screaming silence, and never leaves our side. But, although God never leaves us down for the count, it can feel as if He comes frighteningly close to walking away. I have felt the last strand of hope pull as far as it will stretch—near the breaking point—before peace came raining down. Perhaps that's what it takes for certain stubborn, type-A, I-can-make-it-aloners! Maybe learning to trust God takes this kind of eleventh-hour faith where our hearts break open, allowing God's grace to permeate our lives and become real.

Cee

BEFORE THAT DECADE OF MY LIFE, I had a predetermined set of expectations. Raised in a godly home and in a strict, legalistic church, surrounded by loving parents and friends, I was headstrong and naïve in my vision of how the drama of my personal life would unfold. Divorce would never be a chapter written into my life story. Single parenthood was a situation for weak, messed-up people. I was happy, and thought clinical depression was for other people—something that you had like the flu, like Jack Nicholson experienced in the movie *One Flew Over the Cuckoo's Nest*. I knew nothing of grace, knew only of the "rules" put in place that were supposed to safeguard me from the messier experiences that tripped up the less enlightened. In my lifeless theology, I believed that if I did "A" and worked hard for "B" then God would be there to finish with "C." Little did I know what was around the corner.

Despite my church's condemnation of the arts, I grew up playing the piano, acting in local theater productions and in commercials, and modeling. I was trying to find "my gig." One pivotal day when I was in my mid-20s I was invited to sing background vocals for a young girl named Amy Grant, who was set to go out on her first tour with a band. Standing onstage with Amy, I experienced the joy of performing in my first Christian concert. I was flooded with gratitude as I realized I could become a part of a community of artists who used their gifts to represent their faith. I went on to sing with Russ Taff, and I started a comedy group called "Ariel."

In the early '80s, I met Melodie Tunney and Marty McCall, and we formed the singing group First Call. We started with a bang: touring with Sandi Patty and recording the first of what would be 12 projects in a 15-year ministry. At last I was a successful musician with a popular Christian vocal group and had, I believed, a rock-solid career. First Call produced 10 projects in 10 years, winning three Dove Awards, "Best New Artist," and then "Group of the Year" twice, as well as five Grammy nominations. First Call was a passion of my heart, and I poured all of my creative energy into the ministry. We were flying high, and I believed First Call's work was untouchable by failure.

Then the rug was pulled out from under me.

First Call fell apart in a season in my life when the messiness of my divorce was still raw, and the impact of my personal healing still very uncertain. Amid controversy, we lost Marabeth Jordan, who had replaced Melodie, and all our hearts were broken. I realized how vulnerable we were to the same issues that seek out and destroy other relationships, marriages, and friendships.

So at the age of 35, I was a single parent with two small children. I was lost in a dark fog as to who I was as a woman and a Christian. Every morning, I woke up and struggled through another agonizing day of trying to make sense of the stress, finances, hormones, and fragments of failed relationships.

At one time, I was sure that if I found myself this broken, God would have no choice but to send me hurtling like flaming toast into the nearest abyss! But here I was. My terrible trouble came packaged as an unwanted divorce, single parenthood, the loss of my music ministry, clinical depression, and financial chaos.

Cle

I CALL MYSELF A RECOVERING BASKET CASE, because that's the honest truth. I'm a poster child for a bumpy, messy life. During the ten years of attempting to adjust to circumstances I never imagined having to face, I fell down flat on my face over and over again. Failure moved in. I lived daily in fear of loneliness, of never being loved again—the aching reality of singleness tormented my dreams. At a certain point I just caved in, and I became very familiar with the condition of clinical depression. I felt more and more like I might end up in one of those psychiatric hospitals, staring out the barred windows, longing for death.

Tragically, divorce, single parenthood, and depression are so commonplace in our culture that they may almost appear to fall short in meeting the criteria for "terrible trouble" category. But I know firsthand now why God hates divorce—

because it tears apart commitments, dreams, and the lives of innocent children.

Where once I was judgmental, my circumstances have granted me empathy. Now I relate to the vulnerable, frightened faces of single parents. When someone loses a job, I understand their fear and their concern about simple things, such as how to feed their family. I have lived through the terror of depression and the fight for life—literally, for the will to have some fight left. I remember how lonely I was, how much I prayed for another chance at marriage, how I was left at the end of myself, wondering if God had turned His back on me as a lost cause. I can still recall the bitterness of feeling forsaken.

If I ever forget, all I have to do is look at my old journal entries, such as this one:

May 1997

Such a dark struggle going on in the most vulnerable places of my heart. Intense moments of utter despair, disheartening waves of doubt that I will ever be out of debt. Fear that this endless traveling—leaving my children sleeping in their rooms while I fly off before dawn across the country to sing about a faith that at times feels hopeless—is madness!

I fight against the tide of loneliness.

I am so angry at God! I just want to punch Him— pound on Him—ask Him why He doesn't hear my prayers. Yet, I know in the midst of feeling this that He does hear—I just do not see. Psalm 147—"His pleasure is in those who fear Him, who wait for His true love."

It strikes me now that the "sweet-bye-and-bye," promised-land-someday, pie-in-the-sky theology does little to quench the burning sting of pain here and

> *now. I can't even imagine the new heaven! I've got so much on my earthly plate. I don't doubt where I am ultimately headed...I just grieve the loss of where I am.*

Because I have walked through my dark valley, I have a passion to reassure others with messy lives about God's love. As Anne Graham Lotz so beautifully puts it, "It's when the Red Sea is before you, the mountains are on one side of you, the desert is on the other side, and you feel the Egyptian army closing in from behind that you experience His power to open an escape route. Power to do the supernatural, the unthinkable, the impossible."

Standing with my back to the waters, alone and crying out to God, I turned the corner from despair and began my journey toward peace. I gave up. I let go of everything I had ever envisioned my life holding. I laid down every dream, every prayer, and every desire for relief before God and cried out loud—

> *I embrace the "No!" I choose to believe that You are God and You are the Father of my children and the Husband of my heart. Although your silence is deafening, I will find peace there. I know You hear my prayers, and You say you are not slow to answer, so I will live with joy in the "no's." Where You are, there is holiness. So I will lay down every treasure I have held to so tightly and find holiness in the places You have me. If I am broken and alone, and all looks like loss, I will believe that You will bring me out of this time in a stronger state of intimacy with You and Your Son than I have ever known.*

I wrote a pivotal song about this bungee-jump of faith called "The Day I Lay My Isaac Down." Realizing that dreams clutched too tightly become idols, I let go of my dreams and took a free-fall leap of faith into the abyss so I could trust in the character of God. My crash site was my salvation— because it was there that I finally broke apart and let in the mercy of Christ.

What appeared to be the end—was the beginning.

"Death is destroyed forever in victory."
Death, where is your victory?
Death, where is your pain?
Death's power to hurt is sin, and the power of sin is the law.
But we thank God!
He give us the victory through our Lord Jesus Christ.

1 CORINTHIANS 15:54-55

Chapter Two

A SISTER NAMED SANDY

Sandy's Story

WHEN CANCER FIRST INVADED HER WORLD, Sandy Tice had three children, a strong, loving husband named Mike who coached basketball, an extended family who adored her, and a spirit that would not lie down and roll over. When Mike and Sandy were married, they never imagined the impact of the vows they took—"In sickness and in health...'til death do us part."

Twelve years after they had spoken those vows, Sandy detected a tiny spot on her breast. After a surgical procedure to remove the lump and a thorough examination of her lymph nodes, the doctors decided that, after she had gone through a series of radiation treatments, she would be fine.

But literally five weeks shy of the five-year mark—which the American Cancer Society says is the time when a cancer patient can fully exhale and assume a clean bill of health for the future—Sandy began to have pain in her sternum and shoulder. Three doctors misdiagnosed her. She was treated for arthritis and bursitis with steroids. It was not until, providentially, a bone oncologist at her church asked her to come to his office for another opinion that she discovered she had cancer of the sternum.

Thus began another round of radiation treatments—21 in all. But Sandy wasn't about to miss anything in her life. She rallied to travel to watch her talented daughter Tonya play basketball and earn scholarships and accolades. In 1993, ten years after the first spot was discovered, Mike was coaching a basketball tournament in Texas. Sandy was with him. While she was there, one of her lungs collapsed, and the doctors discovered that aggressive cancer had moved into the lining of her lungs. Sandy bravely faced more surgery.

Ⓒℓℓ

SANDY'S YOUNGER SISTER, NANETTE, told me about her sister's reaction. "Sandy was mad and upset. She was nervous, not so much because of the cancer, but because she didn't want lung surgery to mess up her ability to sing! She loved to sing, and nothing was going to stop her from singing as long as she lived!"

Fortunately, Sandy's voice remained as strong and beautiful as ever. Through the messy, horrible burden of cancer that she bore, you can see the truth of amazing grace of the love of Jesus. He was her captain in battle, her strength in weakness, and allowed her to keep the gift she loved so much—the music she found such solace and comfort in.

Her children were a constant source of support and saw in their mother's brave-hearted faith the reality of a Jesus who was ever-present with them, a Christ who understood pain and had overcome death. In their faces you can now see the beauty of what Sandy and Mike gave them—something that no cancer could rob them of. Their lives were full to the brim and overflowing, in the midst of a very messy world.

"My mother has had cancer since I was 11 years old," Sandy's oldest daughter, Tonya, told reporter Kristy Franklin of the Macon, Georgia, *Journal Record*. "We have grown up with it. But because of my mother and cancer we have learned to depend on God more. She has helped us establish a foundation we can lean on in tough times."

To these comments Sandy added, "The cancer has been tough on my kids…But because of this I have seen them grow spiritually. It has taught them God is in control of everything and He allows everything to happen. The kids probably grew up before their time. But they are more compassionate because of it."

Every year of Sandy's life she valued as a miracle. Each goal she made with her husband, Mike, and their family, was a milestone to celebrate. "We were always trying to get through something," Mike said. "Her first goal was to see her children graduate high school." Sandy's two daughters, Tonya and Amanda, and her son, Chad, gave their mother the joy of accomplishing this goal.

Not only did Sandy live to see her babies grow up and graduate, she lived to see them marry and grow into wonderful adults, and she was able to enjoy holding their babies.

Nanette recalled how Sandy willed herself to live until she was ready to let go. Nothing could keep her down. One day, before having a major treatment, she was up and singing at a service she refused to miss. Her performance put skin and bones and blood and guts to a faith that believes in what cannot be seen. Her voice never wavered. Her gaze out at the crowd was intensely sure. She wore a new head wrap that day but looked stunningly beautiful. God gave Sandy an inner light, one that shone through her dying body. Watching her, you know that this was not the final chorus. We'd see this lady again!

Sandy said, "A lot of times I do not even think about having cancer. It has never kept me from doing anything I wanted to do. I can say cancer has changed my life for the better. It has opened a lot of doors for me to help others."

Tonya wrote a letter to nominate her mother for the 1999 American Life Inspiration Award given by the American Cancer Society. About her mother, she wrote:

> *When my mother is not fighting a battle herself, she is reaching out to others who are involved in this same war. A specific situation that comes to mind took place a few weeks ago. My mother had just started a new treatment…the treatment left her with days of difficult side effects. During this period, a friend and member of my mother's church was diagnosed with breast cancer. When Mother heard this, she somehow managed enough energy to go visit her friend. She stayed with her for about two hours, educating her and comforting her. When Mother got home, she was exhausted; I am sure that her friend had no idea how badly my mother was feeling. Mother has reached out to several women in the community who have breast cancer. My mother has such compassion for people who are in this war…sharing her experience, her time, and her talents—giving what she gives best—herself.*

Sandy won the award.

By May 2000, Sandy's condition was rapidly worsening. The cancer spread to her liver, her spinal column, and at last, as her sister, Nanette, said, "to the place we had all prayed it would never go, to her brain." Nanette agonized over her sister's decline. They had planned a trip to Hawaii, and she didn't know what to do. Should she cancel the trip? The doctors all declared that Sandy could not survive it.

Everyone underestimated this sister named Sandy.

Nanette was astounded to find that Sandy was packed and ready to go to Hawaii, right on schedule. When I later looked at photos, I saw Sandy's face smiling and radiant as she sat with her family. Not a woman to miss anything she had her heart set on, she drank in every second of the loveliness of the islands and refused to let the cancer keep her happiness bottled up.

By October, Sandy had undergone the strongest chemotherapy treatments available. Both of the top cancer centers in the U.S.—in Houston and Boston—would not admit her because the cancer had reached stage four. (This is the final period, in which the disease spreads to the body's organs.) The goals now set were for short periods of time, and were simple. The family prayed that Sandy would make it to Thanksgiving. Then to her favorite time, Christmas.

"Sandy *loved* Christmas—I mean, she went all out!" Nanette told me. "There were trees everywhere and every kind of decoration you could imagine. She would just go crazy! She just had the greatest time with presents, hiding things, and surprises, and we wanted so much for her to make it through Christmas that year."

But Sandy weakened every day. Still this woman of God, this woman of faith, did not seem afraid of the death that was coming. Her daily visits for radiation treatments were usually followed by trips to Wal-Mart. "She wanted to go shopping every day," Mike remembers. "She just had to get ready for Christmas."

Sandy was also preparing for death.

"She once told me not to lie around and cry or crawl into a hole," her husband says. "She told me to get back into my life. She told me that if I didn't, she would come back to haunt me! And then she said to always keep a smile on my face, be happy, and to tell someone I love them."

Sandy made preparations for her funeral as if she were planning a wedding. She knew she was going home to the arms of Jesus, and so she wanted things done a certain way so her death would be celebrated just as she had celebrated her life. She left a list of who would be her pallbearers, what music should be played, and what flowers to order.

"She hated carnations…We had to have white roses, only white—but never carnations. They were out of the question," Nanette said, smiling.

Sandy died at 10:50 A.M. on Christmas Eve day, at the age of 49. Her last words were, "I'm going to win…I'm going to beat this." I believe that she did.

⟶⟵

AT FIRST, NANETTE RECALLS FEELING horribly frustrated that her sister had died right before Christmas, hours before her favorite holiday. Then Nanette thought of how her older sister had always lived life on her own terms, despite the disease, and she now believes that she went home to God on her own timetable.

"When I think about it, Sandy wanted to be in heaven for the biggest Christmas party of all," Nanette said. "She wasn't about to miss out on being with Jesus and God and all the angels on Christmas morning. It was absolutely perfect timing, just as she would have planned it."

Sandy never completed the memory books she'd prepared for each of her children, for Nanette, and for her husband. After her death, Mike found a notebook of poems she had written about herself that she had kept private, even from him, and also poems to surround the memory-book pictures. Mike summoned the courage to finish the memory books for his wife after her death. Looking through Nanette's book, I saw Sandy's love and warmth and strong faith. Reading the words she had left for Nanette, seeing the pictures and poetry, and the way in which she saw herself held in the hands of Jesus, I could see that Sandy had lived and died fully aware that she was truly not alone, was never abandoned, and was maybe even given a special measure of Christ's grace in the most cruel moments of her life.

This lady knew God. She loved Christ. And she lived out the miracle of a spirited life—enjoyed, inhaled, taken in, no matter what the state of her physical body. Sandy was a testament to triumph through suffering. A warrior against pain and defeat, this mother and grandmother did not give in or give up. She, at last, simply said good-bye.

God must have met her in death with His very real presence and love. Her faith made her death seem like a beginning.

Before Sandy's death, her daughter Tonya said, "I pray I can be half the mother, friend, and godly servant my mother is. She has leaned on God and allowed Him to touch everyone around her. She used her time on earth to reach out to others."

I share with you the story of a sister named Sandy as certain proof that Jesus will never leave us alone—however messy, however grim the forecast. His love truly casts out fears of abandonment, even in death. Sandy lived life to the fullest—beautiful and full of laughter, love, and strength. No matter the heavy weight of her burden, her faith ran deeper than the cancer she endured for 17 years. When she left this messy world, she left it changed by her courage and her faith.

*Faith like Job's cannot be shaken
because it is the result of having been shaken.*

RABBI ABRAHAM HESCHEL

Chapter Three

BLESSINGS FROM CURSES

Job's Wife

IN THE LAND OF UZ LIVED JOB, *a God-fearing man with a wife, seven sons, three daughters, and a host of amenities: cattle, land, wealth, houses. He was put to the test in what seems to us like a bizarre cosmic chess game between God and Satan.*

God allowed Satan to test this blameless man's faith in every way save taking his life. In this story, we see the strength of Job's belief in the ultimate goodness of God. We also read of this valiant man's effort to question God while suffering unthinkable torment, the onslaught of the advice of well-meaning friends, and the suggestion of his wife that he "curse God and die!"

Much has been written about Job and his responses to this brutal trial. Yet, I wonder about Job's wife. Little is written about her and what she endured. Could it be that her responses to life embody the primal reasons Christ went to the cross—to take upon His heart her broken heart? If we had a record of her emotional outcries, I think it might look like this…

"Job! I cannot bear this another day! Who do you think you are to take this abuse, after the sinless life you've lived before God?" I railed and screamed at my husband to curse God and die. I begged him to give up. Years of living faithful lives had brought down on our heads nothing but death, destruction, and agony. The years of sacrifices and prayers had proved little good in the end!

Somewhere in my mind, I had assumed that walking a life of honor before God would tip the scales of justice in our favor. In my naivete, I had imagined that an invisible canopy of protection shielded our lives, the land, the children, and the future.

Then came the startling day of truth. All was lost. There was no barrier between good and evil. They conspired and coexisted together in the very midst of our home. Why had Job been leading our family in fasting, prayers, and a humble life before Yahweh? It mattered nothing to God! All of our faith ran through the fingers of the Almighty like grains of sand. All for nothing—nothing!

God had turned a deaf ear to our cries for help, and my husband at last lay dying an agonizing death in front of me.

"Our children have all been taken from us in one night! My seven sons—my three daughters—murdered in a blood-bath in one cruel hour! Our entire lives have been destroyed senselessly! Where is God when we need Him? He is nowhere to be found! Enough already!" I spit on God and all He had allowed my dear husband to lose, and for allowing me to lose so much as well.

My children and family, my life and home—all lost so quickly for no reason. My babies, my sons and daughters. How I ached to the bone! My mother's heart was wounded to the core. When I heard the news of their deaths, it was impossible to even take it in. At first, I was numb. Then, each breath I inhaled seemed more painful than the one before. Not true...not true...some mistake...my mind was spinning...my head pounding...not my babies, my children, my life!

Not like this!

I rushed to the place they had been killed; I had to see with my own eyes my precious family. Crushed, gone, their youthful bodies silenced by death. Oh, how I longed to wrap my arms round them, to hear their laughter, to smell the scent of their clothing. Flooded with memories of their childhood, their first steps, first words, their parties, watching them learn to ride our horses, running through our fields. The peace on their faces as Job and I tucked them into bed at night.

Insanity surged through me. At one point, a friend who was with me stopped me from dashing my head upon the stones that had crushed my children. The madness of grief was followed by a soul slowly turning to ice. There was no comfort, no faith, no reason to live, no will to put one foot in front of the other.

Then came the oceans of anger. I screamed to the Lord our God with such force, such rage, such begging for answers... At last I literally had no voice. No sound. No ability to cry. It was as if I too had died with my family.

My Job was of little help to me, for his losses were compounded by the boils and sickness that ravaged his body. Were they symptoms of his grief? Had he willed a plague upon himself for all that happened?

Only one thing seemed clear. God was not our friend. He was not to be trusted. He had become my enemy. That is why I asked Job to turn his back on God and die. Yet, the faith of my husband would not die. Truth be told, he did curse the day he was born. He questioned God, begging for answers to our misery. All the while my Job—he put up with those "friends" who kept coming to him with their answers all wrapped up, tied with tidy, pious bows.

I hated them as much as I did God. Easy for *them* to interpret our predicament. At night they left us to go back home to their families, homes, and health. We lived with immovable grief.

And it was beyond unbearable to watch my husband suffer so. But oh, how wrong I was…just as self-righteous in my own small-minded reasoning as anyone I might have condemned. Job's friends and I had much in common, each of us interpreting a God whose mysteries defy interpreting, defy containment. For in the end, God did speak to my Job, and with such force and power that we fools, we babblers, were both completely silenced.

God is God. We are not. His ways cannot be judged according to our limited vision. Job's faith was beaten, but never once did he blame God, which is more than I can say for myself. I was so terribly angry, and I made everything so much worse for Job by my venomous attitude. If only words were visible and could be whisked out of the air after they've been spoken…

Yet, God restored to me children—I saw the birth of ten more! With great mercy He forgave me through the prayers of my husband, and blessed us with ten times what had been taken from us. We lived to hold grandchildren and great-grandchildren. They ran and played and grew up before us, each face a reminder of God's love. Through the wounds my husband bore, many have seen true faith in action. God's ways, thankfully, go far beyond our own. He never allows one tear or moment to be wasted.

How can One so terrifying and merciful be One who is so forgiving and holy?

JOB'S WIFE'S REACTIONS TO HER LOSSES *leave me squirming a bit. When my life fell apart, I too fell into a place of doubting God's love and even His presence. Perhaps out of fear, I refused to blame God for my divorce, loneliness, single-parenting, dating disasters, and depression. But parts of my heart, like that of Job's wife, were swept into a self-protective space where I began to believe I was beyond help. It was easier to accept the diagnosis of "too late" for my life than to open myself up to further pain by allowing hope a place to grow.*

Still, as God's mercies dawn new every morning, so did His pursuit of my heart continue to push down the barriers of doubt I attempted to erect. Like Job's wife, more was allowed into my life than I had dreamed or imagined. Nothing had been wasted. And as only God can do, He used the pain intended to deaden my soul's dreams to break into a deeper place than I knew existed—a place where there was birthed a passion to know God, to love and trust Him more in spite of my circumstances.

Now I can take that which was meant for destruction in my life and use it to share my hope with others in this world who lie bleeding by the road. I understand the valleys—so with a grateful heart, I can celebrate the mountains.

Admitting to the Mess

In short, Jesus honored the dignity of each person whether he agreed with him or not. Anyone, even a half-breed with five husbands or a thief nailed to a cross, was welcome to join his kingdom. The person was more important than the category.

PHILIP YANCEY,
from *Finding God in Unexpected Places*

Chapter Four

GOD IN THE DIRT

Bonnie's Story

ALL PARENTS WONDER HOW THEY WILL respond when their child asks the really "big" questions about life. When I was divorced and was left as a single mother, I prayed for God to give me wisdom in answering my daughter and son when those questions came up. They almost always came out of nowhere, while we were riding in the car. I wish I had had a video camera installed in my car to capture the "deer caught in the headlights" look in my eyes as my wide-eyed babes would turn and ask me to explain to them the unexplainable. Thankfully, I would have to concentrate on driving while I was talking about the birds and the bees, politics, divorce, friendships, and other multifarious topics.

When my son, Graham, was five years old, he bounded into the car after school one afternoon and asked me, "Where is God?" Thrilled at his enthusiastic question, I launched into a dissertation on creation and the universe and gave an illustrative description of the majesty of God's astounding handiwork. I told Graham about how God gave His Son Jesus to us and how all things are held together in Christ. Finally, I finished my speech by exclaiming, "Graham, God is everywhere!"

Graham's big blue eyes lit up. "He's everywhere?" he asked incredulously.

This was exciting. An epiphany. I figured this moment was much like when Helen Keller's teacher, Annie, broke through into the silent and dark world that Helen inhabited, and Helen finally connected the water rushing over her hands with the alphabet language Annie had been teaching her. Graham would finally understand how God inhabits our world.

"Well, Mom, if God is everywhere..." Graham hesitated, then went on triumphantly, "then God is in my nose!"

Stunned, I was unable to find any kind of rebuttal to his incredibly simple theological reasoning. Graham had *me* by the nose. He continued: "God is in my elbow! He's in my ears! He's in my hair and fingers and my belly button!"

I piously tried to turn the conversation toward the broader concepts of God's creation. "Graham, God made your body, but He's also in the trees and sky and will live in your heart and spirit..." Graham wasn't buying it.

"But Mom, you said He's everywhere! He's even in the car door!"

Nightmares of Shirley MacLaine's New Age philosophy started to crawl through my head. "No, Graham, God is not in the car door—" I was cut off by Graham, who pulled up his pants leg and leaned over to scratch his leg.

Grinning, he looked up at me, admitting, "I do feel a little bit weird now when I have to 'itch' Him."

Many times since that day, I have replayed the conversation in my mind, wishing I had answered Graham with a different explanation. Perhaps this one: "Graham, the reason we are here is that in the beginning of time, God liked to

play in the dirt. Where is God? He's usually found somewhere playing in the dirt." I'm almost certain that such an
answer would have thrown my talkative son into a short-
lived silence.

"God plays in the mud?" Graham might have asked.

And I would have answered, "Yes...God began playing in
the mud the day He made Adam and Eve from the dirt of the
ground in the Garden of Eden. He's never been afraid of getting His hands dirty when it comes to His children. He's not
afraid of the mud or of cleaning us up when we get muddy."

Graham had a favorite mud puddle that he played in for
weeks. I have no clue what drew him to this particular wet
spot, but he would throw rocks into it, build piles of sticks in
it, and then show up at the front door covered with grime,
telling me oh-so-innocently, "Mom I don't know *how* I got so
dirty!" Of course, Graham didn't see me looking through the
window, watching him play in the mud. I knew he would
come in, prime candidate for a Tide commercial and in need
of a good hosing-down.

I am reminded of how God watches me as I play in the
mud in my own way—rolling in the dirt, making piles of
rubbish, or fighting my way through them. Some of those
piles have been of my own making, and others were filled
with the garbage of bad theology, legalism, and the betrayals
and lies of others. Eventually, no matter what causes the disarray, I am a prodigal daughter who can only pray, "Lord, I
don't know how I made such a mess of things, or how things
have gotten so ugly. Can You help me out of this? Can I be
washed again with Your grace and understanding? I can't
clean up my act alone."

Throughout the Bible, I find comfort in God's tenacious,
fearless love. Over and over again He comes in and cleans up
the messes we find ourselves in. We are really good at getting

ourselves stuck in the mud, but God's hand continually reaches out with grace to pull us out.

THE ACCOUNT OF THE WOMAN CAUGHT in adultery in John's Gospel, chapter 8, is a staggering example of God—through His Son, Jesus—literally playing in the dirt. Obviously, this is one very messy lady, caught in the act, caught in a sin that required her to be put to death according to the Old Testament law.

I picture her being dragged through the town to the edge of the city, terrified and filthy, shame-ridden and lacking any sense of self-esteem, trembling as she awaited her death at the hands of an angry mob. One could ask, where was the guilty man she was caught with? The Bible account does not mention his fate or where he may have scurried off to hide. This woman was left alone to bear the consequences of the sins of both of them.

But it seems that one of Jesus' missions on Earth was to reestablish God's love for women. In the Jewish culture of that day, women were easily discarded, often punished and divorced at the whim of their husbands. They were second-class citizens. Jesus repeatedly went out of His way to set the record straight and to show God's love for His daughters.

Insults and rude remarks flew through the air, and all eyes were on the adulteress. She awaited the death blows of the stones. Yet Jesus didn't speak. Rather, He sat down and began to write in the dirt with His fingers. Calmly, quietly, with this unsettlingly simple act, Jesus took the attention off the accused woman and onto Himself. Then He made the show-stopping comment: "Anyone here who has never sinned can throw the first stone at her."

The Bible says that after this Jesus bent down and again wrote in the dirt. All the questions that were thrown at Him about keeping the law of Moses—which required her death—were suddenly silenced. Who knows what Jesus was drawing there in the dirt? Here was God, once more having His way with His hands on the earth, giving new life to one who had no hope. Evidently the words of Jesus caused the stone-throwing mob to remember some of their own muddier, sinful moments. Stones dropped, the shuffling, disgruntled men made their exit. The tension dissipated. Jesus was left alone with the broken, trembling woman.

"Where are your accusers?" Jesus asked.

"They are all gone," the woman told Him.

"Then I will not accuse you either," Jesus said. "Go and sin no more."

After this, as often is the case throughout the Bible, there is no description of how this woman's life changed. She went back into the city whose men had condemned her, and perhaps she rebuilt her self-esteem and made right the wrongs she had committed. Perhaps she asked forgiveness. Surely she walked with her head held a little bit higher, feeling loved by God through His Son—One she did not know yet could not deny, because He had saved her life.

Jesus said that when we see Him, we see God. This means that the Creator of the universe is unafraid to get right into the middle of shameful situations—messy, dirty places—places that He understands because He did not shield Himself from experiencing them together with His people. God can be found everywhere, from my son's nose to sitting alongside of a condemned adulteress. From the dust and dirt of this Earth He redeems and teaches and loves us through the messiness of life, unafraid to play in the dirt with us, giving love a chance to change our world.

Nicole Johnson said it well in *Dropping Your Rock*. She wrote of our messes,

> *These are drop-your-rock moments. Love is giving us a chance to choose. Grace doesn't just let us off; it sets us free. With one blow it strikes the shackle, breaking it open so we may walk unfettered in freedom. It promises us a better tomorrow than the today we've made for ourselves. "Go and sin no more." The "go" is the grace.*

Prostitutes are in no danger of finding their present life so satisfactory that they cannot turn to God: the proud, the avaricious, the self-righteous, are in that danger.

C.S. Lewis

Chapter Five

FROM THE MESS COME THE MESSENGERS

Regina's Story

I OFTEN THINK THAT IF JESUS were making His way through Nashville, Tennessee, He'd always make time to stop by Magdalene House and bring in with Him a few new messy, broken women to leave there. One woman He might have brought in is Regina. Recently, she shared her story with me.

Regina was raised in church but couldn't wait until she was old enough to quit attending. When she was 17, she left home, dropped out of school, and began a wild lifestyle— "going crazy," as she puts it. Soon Regina was pregnant, and she quickly got married—to a physically and emotionally abusive man. She finally convinced him to abandon her by threatening him with the lie that her father was going to throw him out. But Regina's father was an alcoholic who sold drugs, so going back home wasn't a good option. Her mother ignored her husband's addictions and adhered to a legalistic lifestyle, railing at her children about which denomination of church they attended and why.

It's no wonder that when someone introduced Regina to drugs and prostitution, it looked like a promising escape.

Regina remembers it this way. "I met this guy who introduced me to the streets. I was curious, you know—I'd never been allowed to have company or go anywhere, and my husband had been so abusive. After he left I went to South Eighth Street, and it was *rockin'* up there! I had come from such a strict home and strict husband, and I was like 'Curious George' about life. I felt like a kid when I showed up on the street, and it looked like everybody was having fun."

It was there Regina met a man who was counting the money he'd just made from a drug sale. Soon she was selling marijuana, then other drugs, making a lot of money. "I was happy, starting to have things, to do things," Regina remembers. She now had a young son to take care of, and drugs seemed to be the perfect way to support them both.

Regina's life went from bad to worse. She began living with another drug dealer, and although they never married, he and Regina had two sons together. Then, a drug deal went bad, and he was killed. Regina was devastated. In the depths of despair, Regina turned to cocaine.

"Crack cocaine was the most destructive drug I ever put into my system," Regina recalls. "That's the con of it. The first time I tried it I thought it was such a waste of money—I didn't even feel high and wondered why anyone would buy this stuff! But then it's in your system and you don't realize what you've done. It's like you've allowed a spirit to come in and it lies dormant, just waiting for the opportunity to surface, and then you're off to the races."

Regina was hooked. In 1994 she was arrested and sentenced to six months in jail on her first drug conviction. Her children went to live with her mother while Regina served her term. When Regina was released, she immediately went back to the streets.

REGINA NEEDED MONEY FOR HER HABIT, so she turned to prostitution. Soon, she was turning tricks for as little as $5, or sometimes up to $200, "just to get a hit. Stupid me," she said ruefully. In her desperation, she tried prayer. "I'd say, 'God, please help me, I can't do it, but I know You can! I want to stop but I don't know how and I'm scared. I'm scared I'm going to die out here. You're sitting up there, looking down here, and You need to do something!' I'd cuss and pray and get high—and cuss and pray, 'God, sittin' up there on Your high throne, You see this, You need to help me!' and then I'd take another hit off my pipe."

Regina bounced in and out of jail, usually for six months at a stretch. Then one morning Regina was walking the streets, looking for a "date" so she could have enough money for more drugs. She saw a man in a hardware parking lot, and he invited her to get into his van. But the man, who introduced himself as "Rodney," didn't want a date. He wanted to buy her breakfast. Rodney began talking about Jesus, and he asked Regina if she knew how much Jesus loved her. Both he and his wife, Mazey, were recovering heroin addicts, and he wanted Regina to hear about what God had done for them. Then he told Regina he wanted to take her home to meet his wife.

Regina remembers wanting to jump out of the van, but she told me she believes an angel kept her from being able to open the doors—even though they were unlocked! Before she could figure out a way to escape, they had reached Rodney's home.

"He pulled up to his house and out runs this pregnant lady with these little kids and she says to me, 'Oh, you precious baby!'" Regina said. "She didn't know me! I thought these people were crazy! 'It's gonna be all right,' she kept telling me, and then she hugged me."

By this time Regina was crying, and Jesus was showing her that this was what she had prayed for. She was tired of life on the street. Tired of prostituting herself. She missed her children. She was ready to change.

Rodney and Mazey invited her into their house, heedless of the potential danger this drug-addicted prostitute presented. *"This has got to be God,"* Regina remembers thinking. *"God is doing this.* I couldn't fight fight against it. Most of me didn't want to fight against it."

Mazey asked, "Regina, what do you want?" Regina told her, "A hit!" and laughed. But then she broke down and admitted she didn't want to keep living the way she had been. "Baby, don't worry about it," Mazey told her. "God loves you."

Then she and Rodney and their kids gathered around Regina. Together, they called out the spirits of addiction and prostitution. "Suddenly I fell to the floor and this warm feeling came over me and I couldn't get up! It was wonderful! When I was able to get up, I felt so drained and clean."

Regina got out her purse and laid out the contents: condoms, razor blades, drug paraphernalia. There were no pictures of her or her family; nothing that would tell anyone about who she was as a person.

"You just throw all that away," Mazey told Regina. "God is going to give you everything new." Regina began crying as Mazey and Rodney said that God had told them to help her, and that she was to stay with them. For months she lived with these parents for prodigals and allowed the Holy Spirit to teach her the truth. Regina puts it this way: "It wasn't like anything I'd heard at church growing up, it wasn't anything Rodney or Mazey said—but I spent quiet time with my

Bible and the Holy Spirit taught me. I was getting strong in the Spirit and I knew this was real!"

Full of joy that God had answered her prayers, Regina remembered a vow that she and the other prostitutes had made to each other. "If you guys make it out of this hellhole before me, please don't leave me here. Please come back for me. And if I make it out, I'm going to come back and tell you what I've found."

℃

DESPITE WARNINGS FROM HER new Christian friends that she wasn't ready, Regina was determined to go back to the streets and try to rescue her friends. It wasn't long before she was sucked back into her old life. It started when a "friend" she was witnessing to insisted that Regina "take a hit" while praying with her. Regina convinced herself that she was covered by the blood of Christ and would be able to handle it. She knew she was a child of God. Yet, Regina remembers, "I kept going back to the devil's playground." First it was the hit. Then smoking "just one joint," then drinking "just one beer." Before she knew what was happening, Regina was back to prostitution. And devastated by the guilt and shame she felt.

Regina's life spiraled down into desperation. In and out of jail, she promised herself each time that she would clean up her life and regain custody of her children. Yet in the end she would turn to the streets as the only place to make money. It was an agonizing cycle of defeat.

Then God did something only God can do. He provided a severe mercy.

Regina and her roommate needed cash. They stole a truck and headed to a local truck stop where they could find some "dates" and earn money for drugs. They were broke, so a worker at a Kentucky Fried Chicken gave them a free meal. Then they drove to a motel, where they tried the doors of the rooms until they found one that opened. They slept, and the next morning they headed for the truck stop. Turned in for using the motel room, they were caught by the police and arrested. By this time, Regina was so desperate that she welcomed the police.

"I wanted to go to jail so bad…I'm thinking, *What do I have to do for you to arrest me, hit one of you guys?*" she remembers. "They thought I was crazy because I was praising God, knowing He had done this. God sent me to jail and I was so happy."

Regina's jail time went by much too quickly. When she was released, she was terrified. She wanted to change, but she knew she was weak—and she didn't have any money to start a new life. Once more, the merciful, unshakable love of Jesus came through. A friend told her about Magdalene House, a place for recovering prostitutes. "It's a recovery house named for Mary Magdalene in the Bible," her friend explained. Regina phoned Sarah Martin, the director of Magdalene House, and was told to come over as soon as she was released. When Regina saw the beautiful home, she was positive that she had gotten the wrong address. Everything was gorgeous and clean and lovely.

She was greeted by several of her friends who she had worked the streets with and served jail time with. "I walked into this house and it was gorgeous," Regina said. "It reminded me of what *home* was. There was *my* bed and it was pretty and nice. I was asking, 'What do I have to do? Nobody is just going to give me this.' "

Then Regina met the founder, Becca Stevens. Becca shattered all of Regina's preconceptions about clergy. "Becca is like Jesus. Her arms are held open wide," Regina said. "Just like Him she says, 'Come on, just like you are, come on. We've got something for you. What do you want to do? We're going to walk beside you and make it happen.'" Magdalene House was infused with the spirit of Jesus Christ. There were no sidelong, judgmental glances here; rather, there was an atmosphere of mercy and compassion, and the possibility of another chance. At Magdalene House, prostitutes are loved through their recovery from drug abuse, helped to build their self-esteem, and counseled about their history of abuse.

Regina went back to school and was able to regain custody of her children. Becca offered her a job with the Magdalene staff, and now Regina's eyes fill with tears of gratitude when she speaks of how she is able to welcome other Magdalene women to a new life.

"I know how it is…We're all feisty and have just come off the streets," Regina said. "I tell them that they have been chosen by God. I tell them they are covered by the blood of Jesus."

❦

AFTER I HEARD HER STORY, Regina and I were both in tears. I hugged this dear woman, this living example of how far the love of Jesus will go to win back each and every one of His daughters. I asked her what she would say to anyone who felt their life was too messy, too far gone, for Jesus to love them.

"Girl, God takes the messiest people and cleans us up from the mess," Regina told me. "He tells us that we are messengers, He says 'Go and tell the world about how messy you were and how now you are My messenger.' We are messengers and messengers come from the messiest of the mess. That's how God works."

As of this writing, Regina has been clean and sober for five years. "I couldn't have done it alone," Regina said. She tells me she thinks about Mary Magdalene. "I think how she went to Jesus and asked for forgiveness and He gave her everything new and a new way of life...and self-respect...There is no shame, no condemnation. Girl, I was on a journey all along and I'd come full circle."

Regina found a path to new life at Magdalene House. After talking with her, I left with a sense of how Jesus must have felt when He saw His grace transform the wretched, tormented women He came in contact with. The work of Jesus in Mary Magdalene—a broken, hurting loser who found love and acceptance and new life at His feet—lives on through Magdalene House—yet another house of God.

Maybe we should look more carefully—look for the people God chooses rather than the people we would choose.

MADELEINE L'ENGLE,
from *The Rock That Is Higher*

Chapter Six

LIVING WATER

The Samaritan Woman

IN JESUS' TIME, SAMARIA WAS A PROVINCE *that was avoided by the Jews if possible. Samaritans were considered hopeless, useless, and unclean. It was here that Jesus reached out to a woman who was in a mess. Married five times, living with a man out of wedlock, she was likely considered the lowest of lowlife in a city already thought to be beyond hope.*

In the town of Sychar, Jesus stopped at the well of Jacob. Tired and weary, He waited for His disciples to return with food. As the Samaritan woman made her daily journey to the well to draw water, she encountered Jesus. Imagine her surprise when Jesus asked her for a drink! Jews were told to have nothing to do with Samaritans.

Jesus, always drawn to every weak, weary, hopeless woman and man that He met, spoke to her. He told her He had a different kind of water for her. Living water...

I'M A STUBBORN WOMAN. I'm not easily persuaded by pretty language and empty promises. The land of Samaria was what it was. We were second-class citizens—lower, unworthy, left to be leftovers. Jews did not talk to people from my country. We were like dogs to them. They thought they knew so much about the Law of Moses, and they told us that Jerusalem was the only place to worship God—so that left us out in the cold.

I lived my life as I saw fit. Being sentenced to my wretchedness, I took that sentence to its extreme. Men were in the world to be used. They used me, I used them. What did it matter to a dog woman in Samaria?

Still, some part of me thought about the Holy Scriptures and believed that if God were to see the abuse of my people, He would surely be angry. Perhaps He might even do something extraordinary to put things right. After all, our shared history with the Jews could not be changed. We had a well that had been in use since Jacob lived, one that was used by his sons and for his cattle too.

Every day I would go to the very well that Jacob built to draw water. I was told it didn't matter. Our part of the country was defiled. We were looked upon as if we were nothing. If you can imagine this, the Jews were even instructed not to lay hands on the same things that we had simply touched! You would think we were lepers.

The day that Jesus, the Messiah, asked me to give Him a drink from the well, I was shocked. I had heard of this prophet who called Himself the Son of Man. I have to laugh now, for being a woman, and a woman who had little respect for who I was or for anyone else I did not trust this Nazarene. Even the Samaritan men would rarely speak to me unless they wanted something in return. With whispers and gestures to follow them into back alleys and vacant locations they would get me to oblige them, for a price.

So, I thought to myself, *what does this Jesus want? He is a man like all the others I have known, right?* But He began to talk to me just like He would talk to someone He held in high regard. He told me of living water that would soothe my thirst forever. How could He see the drought in my heart? Somehow, Jesus knew everything about me—and yet we had never met. He even knew about the men…the many men…. and the man I was with at that time. Why did His eyes never look at me with hate or disgust? Why did I feel released from my shame?

Men were the ones who initiated divorce in our culture. Five times I had been thrown out, dumped by my husbands, and now I was living with a man in sin. Jesus could easily have condemned me and counted up the ways in which I was unfaithful to the law, all the reasons why I had been rejected.

Instead, He saw that I was thirsty, so very thirsty for more than water…thirsty for a reason to live. He answered my doubting questions with patience in His voice and invited me to drink of His "living water" that would change my life. When I told Him that the Messiah would come one day to explain all of these things—where to worship, and how we might have life everlasting—Jesus the Nazarene told me that He was the One of which I spoke…the Messiah. Yes, He looked me right in the eye and said, "I am He." How could the Messiah be talking to me, a despised, worn-out, useless Samaritan slut? When His followers walked up they were stunned to see Him speaking to me. I know they were thinking He had gone mad. I was used to being looked down on.

Turning to them with a smile, I left. But something inside Jesus' eyes spoke the truth to my heart. I knew I had seen God in Him. Something inside me realized that He wanted more for me, in all my used-up, beaten-down condition.

This Nazarene wanted me to have new life, new water, new self-esteem.

Jesus used me, a Samaritan woman, a user of men, to tell others about His coming. He could have chosen from the many men and women of prominence in Jerusalem. Yet He chose me. Running back to the city to tell everyone about meeting Him, I remembered I'd left my jar at the well.

Who cares? I thought. *I can get it later!* Whether anyone believed what had just happened at Jacob's well or not, it didn't matter. In the deepest well of my heart, I knew I would never be thirsty and never be the same again!

THE WOMAN FROM SAMARIA must have been overwhelmed by all she heard. She recalled the prophetic promises that kept her putting one foot in front of the other in a life that seemed unbearable. "There is a Messiah coming, He will make all things clear!" she insisted. Jesus simply said that He was the One she was waiting to see.

The Samaritan woman was able to bring new hope to her town because of the noonday meeting at the well. She told everyone that she had met an amazing man—a prophet—who knew everything about her, yet had only just met her.

Many people came to find Jesus, and they asked Him to stay with them for another few days. Jesus put His "Day-Timer" obligations on hold. His desire to remain in this forbidden place must have puzzled and frustrated His disciples. But the Samaritans who met Christ declared, "Now we no longer believe (trust, have faith), just because of what you said; for we have heard Him ourselves [personally], and we know that He truly is the Savior of the world, the Christ."

Jesus continually comes to the ones least likely to be noticed, respected, or given hope in our world. When He thanked the Father for showing the innocent and not the wise the truth of His mercy, perhaps it was because the most messy, desperate people need His grace the most.

Learning to Trust God

God crucified formed a bridge between our human perception of a cruelly imperfect and indifferent world and our human need for God, our human sense that God is present...The cross enacts for us deep truths that would make no sense apart from it. The cross gives hope when there is no hope.

PHILIP YANCEY,
from *The Jesus I Never Knew*

Chapter Seven

FAILED EXPECTATIONS

Bonnie's Story

NOTHING QUITE SYMBOLIZES HUMAN expectations put on a rickety pedestal and doomed to failure like the good old all-American "shower"—a party complete with nuts, mints, punch, and silly games. Wedding showers, baby showers, birthday parties, toasts at midnight on New Year's Eve—they all celebrate the expectations of happy moments that await us. We put up elaborate decorations, serve delicious food, and congratulate each other. We buy gifts and offer good wishes.

Celebrations bring to mind the happiness of a new job, the dream-come-true trip, engagement to the perfect soul mate, the white picket fence, or another year's milestone in the life of an accomplished child. Maybe it's a ceremony honoring a high school or college graduation. Perhaps it's a banquet lauding the exploits of athletes, where sports heroes are draped in the colors of their school, state, or country. Applause and cheers punctuate the moments when humans achieve and excel, and enjoy for a time the labor of their hard work.

If only that were how humans' songs were really sung… perfect music composed of uninterrupted soaring melodies and rich harmonies. If only there were not sad laments and discord—things flat, sharp, and just plain out of tune.

If only we never heard the disharmony of dashed expectations.

MY DASHED EXPECTATIONS CAME in many forms, but childbirth in particular was one of the places of starkest disillusionment for me.

Three months into my first pregnancy, I went with my first husband to Chicago so we could visit his brother and a favorite aunt and uncle. It was a glorious day in May. While we were watching the Chicago Cubs playing at Wrigley Field, I started to feel ill, bleed, and experience cramps. Trying to brush aside our fears, we stuck to our schedule. After watching the game, we explored one of the huge museums downtown. I remember seeing a meticulously crafted display of the stages of the human fetus as it grows from month to month. As I looked at the exhibit, my bleeding increased. I was caught in a bad dream. Frightened, I finally sat down on a cold cement bench, and my husband called a doctor. The next two days were spent in and out of Chicago-area emergency rooms.

Not only was I away from my home in Tennessee and having a miscarriage, I was under the care of a Catholic obstetrician who wanted to be absolutely, positively sure my pregnancy was over before performing a D&C. For five days I lay in a hospital bed in painful back labor, my body trying to discharge the fetus that had not formed properly. The doctor would run daily tests to see whether my body was still producing pregnancy hormones. Negative, then positive, then negative, then maybe positive. He refused to take me into surgery until there were at least two concurrent negative tests.

As I lay there in pain, taking medication that would surely have killed any baby, I explored the possible use of a few four-letter words I had yet to ever speak aloud. I called home and cried over the phone, and I had daily visits from my precious aunt and my husband. They both pleaded with the doctor to move ahead with my surgery and felt quite helpless in the situation. We all suffered.

Finally, after a week of massive bleeding, cramping, and waiting, the doctor agreed that it seemed I was indeed having a miscarriage! I was scheduled for a procedure and taken off the pain medication.

As my messy life would have it, on the morning I was slated to be taken to the operating room, a massive automobile pileup occurred on one of Chicago's main freeways. All unnecessary surgeries were put on hold while the hospitals took in seriously injured victims.

So I waited for almost eight hours, clawing at my sheets, crying out in pain, and unable to take anything to calm me. The miscarriage labor was intensely more painful than the two normal labors I experienced later in my life during the birth of my two children. Everything in my body was off-kilter and in trauma. Normal labor is painful, but there is a sense of order to the pain because you are working to produce a living child. By the time I was taken to surgery I was hysterical. The entire experience was a nightmare, but finally it was over.

When I became pregnant with Courtney, I was nervous, but when we passed the 12-week mark with flying colors, I breathed easier. During the baby showers and the anticipation of her arrival, I was immersed in wonder. At one baby shower, as we passed the nuts and mints and drank the punch, I listened to many veteran moms share wisdom, advice, or a prayer for me. It was a sweet time, and visions of a sleeping, chubby-cheeked angel danced in my head.

Not one of these women told me that my child might have colic!

And who would have imagined, as we passed the punch cups at the baby showers, that my baby's collarbone would be broken during a hasty delivery? I don't know why the doctor was in such a hurry. Maybe he had to make a tee time for his golf game, or was late to a lunch appointment, or had something else more important than waiting for my body to be fully ready to deliver. Whatever his reasons, he pulled Courtney from my body using forceps, with such force that he broke her collarbone. My poor baby wailed and cried for three weeks, and I still cringe at the thought of the pain she must have been in before we discovered the problem at her three-week checkup.

My friend Merrill Ann had given birth to her first child, Jonathan, six weeks before me. When she came to visit us at home, I looked at her and demanded, "Merrill Ann! Why in the world didn't you tell me how hard this is?" Courtney cried incessantly with colic. I was a wreck. All the cute little stuffed animals and hanging mobiles and baby toys did little good to calm a wailing daughter and her exhausted mother.

So this was motherhood!

"Well, no one warned me either," Merrill Ann said, and laughed. "I figured you would find out soon enough."

Such is life.

LATER, WHEN I WAS A SINGLE PARENT, there was a time when I longed for a second marriage with such intensity that my prayers for this good thing became an idol. In my loneliness, my broken spirit beat on the doors of heaven for years, until I realized that I had removed God from the throne of my heart and had forgotten to seek His presence first.

When I consider the story of Hannah in the Bible and read about her fervent prayer for a child, I find that it wasn't until Hannah promised the Lord that she would give back the dreams of her heart to Him that He moved on her behalf. When she was willing to give God the place of priority in her heart and in her life, He allowed her to have all she had pleaded for.

God is a jealous God. He is a pursuing, passionate lover of all. Even in our best prayers and deepest desires, He wants to remain our greatest love. In my story, I believe that God permitted me to hurt in my loneliness until I learned that only in seeking Him first with all of my heart and soul and mind would I find rest and peace. He was there all the time, hurting with me, loving me with a love that bears pain infinitely longer than can be imagined. God's love, pouring through the lonely life of Jesus, runs deeper, wider, and farther than any loneliness of the human heart. Prayers from our lonely, troubled lips mix with the prayers of the risen Christ on our behalf. He understands our expectations—and our grief when those expectations fail to materialize.

We look at marriages, births, awards, and other milestones and achievements as the glory moments in the human story. But what do we do when the marriages become difficult, the babies aren't born healthy, the awards cost us more than we counted on, and the perks don't fill the gaping open wounds in our souls?

Simply put, messiness is part of the equation here on this side of paradise. It began in the Garden of Eden when we chose to challenge God's plans, and disobedience led to disarray. We weren't created to understand evil. That's God's territory. Yet, the tree bearing good also held the poison of evil. One bite from the forbidden fruit was all it took to change history.

Thank God that His character and great love couldn't leave us alone in the grip of the enemy. Messy lives weren't part of His passion and plan for His creation. History reveals how God is always coming to us. Coming, always coming, through thick and thin. Coming to be one of us. Coming to be with us. Coming to heal us and to save us from our messy lives. Coming to offer us hope in the midst of our failed expectations.

Our humanity does not separate us from our Father. Rather, it offers us the opportunity to connect with Him— through Jesus, God's heart, God's Son. It offers us the opportunity to be broken but restored. To be hopeful. Because only in Jesus are our expectations truly fulfilled.

"*I live in a high and holy place, but I also live with people who are sad and humble. I give new life to those who are humble and to those whose hearts are broken...I will give peace, real peace, to those far and near, and I will heal them,*" says the LORD.

ISAIAH 57:15,19

Chapter Eight

DESTINY IN THE VALLEY

Diana's Story

I DON'T BELIEVE IN COINCIDENCES.

Diana and I have met twice, with a decade between our encounters. Crossing paths with her is like an intersection with grace. Years ago, when we first met, she worked for a Christian radio station. Ten years later, in completely different surroundings, Diana and I ended up together one muggy afternoon, watching my husband and his friends ride horses on a farm in a remote corner of Tennessee.

Standing off to the side in my new riding boots that had never been worn on a horse, watching accomplished men and women roping little cows' feet, I felt nervous and terribly out of place. I glanced about, clutching my sweaty Diet Coke, and saw Diana sitting on a junky old freezer. *Smart girl, great seat, and there's just enough room on there for the two of us,* I thought, and I introduced myself to her, not recalling our earlier meeting. Settling in for some small talk, I hesitantly shared some of my messy story with Diana, who listened with compassion and interest. I told her how Brent and I had recently married, how God had been faithful to restore my heart and hopes, and how He had taken care of my children.

Diana listened to my story, recalled our first meeting, and then began to catch me up on the details of her life since we'd last met. In the South, when we're stopped short by a piece of information, we often say, "Shut your mouth!" Mine fell open as Diana began to lay out her past, her face peaceful as she described her walk through hell. Sensing me comparing my pain with her pain, weighing them out on the scales of my mind, Diana quietly said, "Bonnie, pain is pain. Whatever brings you to the place of hopelessness levels the playing field. It's all relative."

DIANA GREW UP IN A CHRISTIAN FAMILY and has always been very close to God. For 23 years she was committed to her marriage because of her daughters, Savannah and Mariah, and was loyal to her husband. But her commitment was continually put to the test. When her younger daughter, Mariah, was two, she was riding in a children's wagon and accidentally flipped out of it. She suffered a severe head injury that caused her to become slightly mentally challenged. Mariah's father refused to face what had happened to his daughter and became unable to treat her with the same love and acceptance as he did her older sister, Savannah.

Diana had no idea what she had signed up for in her marriage. Her husband, as she kindly put it, "struggled with anger management." As I would say it, he was verbally and physically abusive to her.

In 1987, Diana was hospitalized for a stroke, which she attributes to medication she was taking for a physical problem. However, it was during this hospital visit that the doctors saw before them a broken woman in need of physical and emotional healing. They told Diana that all the signs pointed toward a major heart attack or stroke in the future if she did not remove herself from the stress of her marriage.

"I was in denial," Diana admits. "They literally had to get in my face and spell out how seriously ill I was. If things continued, I might not fare as well the next time, they said...I could be confined to a wheelchair the rest of my life. I was like a car accident victim who wouldn't believe she was bleeding because there was no mirror to look into. In their way, these doctors held up a mirror so that I could see the damage I'd suffered."

Diana describes her divorce as, literally, a choice between life and death. As a result of this abusive relationship, Diana struggled with low self-esteem.

The one area in which Diana flourished was motherhood. She adored her girls, and they adored her. As the girls entered their teen years, people would see them out together and think the three of them were sisters, laughing, shopping, and giggling.

"People would comment on how much my older daughter, Savannah, and I were alike," Diana told me. "We were almost like identical twins. At one point, we won second place in a mother-daughter look-alike contest."

Diana said that she and Savannah had the same mannerisms, the same voice, and reacted to things like they were twins. "It would be so much fun when her friends would call our house—I'd answer the phone and they would think it was Savannah," Diana said. She added, "Savannah and I were not only mother and daughter, but we grew to be best friends. We would be thinking the same thing and both know it without having to say a word."

Both Savannah and Mariah were pleased when their mom began dating a man she had met at a divorce recovery seminar at a local church. Lee and Diana dated for almost three years—Lee seemed to be an answer to prayer. "I felt so safe with Lee," Diana explains. "I had the security of meeting him in a church, and I liked the tender way he treated me. Lee was soft-spoken, empathetic, and gentle in nature. He had all of the protective qualities my first husband lacked." They got married.

~

IN LESS THAN A YEAR, HER NEW MARRIAGE became a living hell.

Lee worked for a major corporation that had theme stores all across the United States. He traveled extensively in a motor home, sometimes insisting Diana go with him, other times just traveling on his own. "Now I can look back and see the red flags that popped up while we were dating—the ones I disregarded," Diana said. Lee was controlling and manipulative. "He told me when and where I could be, and he dictated my schedule to the minute. But I thought to myself, *This must be normal. I've never known normal.* I interpreted the warning signs in my gut as my being 'gun-shy' about marrying again."

Both Savannah and Mariah were in their twenties and were living in Illinois, close to Diana's relatives, trying to carve out lives of their own. Each daughter carried wounds from growing up in the abusive home of Diana's first marriage. Mariah married a drug addict who abused her both physically and emotionally. He hurried her into her first pregnancy, hoping that it would increase the food stamps and disability money she received so that he could use this additional income to support his drug habit. She was home-less sometimes, and she frequently moved from place to place with her husband, who kept her from having contact with her family.

The final straw for Mariah was when her husband held a knife to her throat and a gun to their infant's head and threatened to kill the baby if she left. Frightened, Mariah took her child and fled home to live with Diana and Lee.

Savannah was also having difficulty. She was living in Chicago with a Christian family and making plans to move into youth ministry. But Diana's first husband also lived in the area, and he began harassing Savannah, a mirror image of her mother, as a means of revenging himself on Diana. In frustration, Savannah phoned Diana and begged her to let her live at home again for a while.

Diana was relieved to have both of her daughters at home, and she delighted in giving her grandson, Colton, her loving attention. For a time, her life seemed to have come a beautiful full circle of redemption.

Yet, destruction was brewing...and Lee's behavior toward Savannah began to reveal his dark side.

"When Savannah moved home, I began to see things," Diana said. "Lee would sit with Savannah on the couch, with his arms around her. Not like a father's touch, more like a boyfriend's. Once, I looked in a mirror and saw them behind me, kissing."

Diana had told Savannah that Lee would be a protective father to her. "I could see her being pulled in by his manip-ulation," she remembers. "He was seducing her and making her feel loved, and she was falling prey to being cared for in this sick way because she'd never known love from a father before."

It was now that Diana began to experience intense anxiety attacks, which escalated into a breakdown and a diagnosis of post-traumatic stress disorder. Still, she tried to be strong for her family, and she began to confront Lee about his behavior with Savannah, as well as caring for her younger daughter and grandson. Lee would never allow Savannah to be alone with Diana. Distance grew between mother and daughter as Savannah fell more deeply under the spell of her stepfather, who treated her with a love she desperately wanted yet knew was somehow wrong.

Diana took a job at a sewing factory to earn money and to try to keep her sanity. She warned Lee that her older daughter was "falling in love" with him. He told Diana he'd take care of the problem his way. When Diana confronted Lee over the lipstick marks she saw on his mouth after he came in the house from talking to Savannah in the driveway, he slapped her.

Mariah began to ask her mom to come home from work early because she sensed something was wrong about Lee and Savannah's relationship. One Sunday, knowing that Lee and Savannah were alone, Diana left church and arrived at home before she was expected. Unable to open the door, which had been dead bolted, she pounded on it; finally she broke the glass, made her way into the house, and found them together. No more denial. No more games.

Diana's arms bear scars from the broken glass. She refers to them as the scars from the day she tried to save her daughter's life. "It was as if my heart were in shreds," Diana said. Her soul was bruised black-and-blue. She was devastated.

Lee told Diana he had been interested in Savannah all along, and this was why he had married her. He then took Savannah, and they moved into the motor home he and

Diana had traveled in. Lee and Savannah lived together on Diana's property for several months.

On the first anniversary of her second marriage, Diana once again collapsed under the weight of sorrow and grief. She was hospitalized for clinical depression. She remembers crying out, "Dear Lord, if you will just help me through this, all I will ever do is speak of your glory, and I will devote the rest of my life to telling every woman I ever meet, every person I know, of your love and kindness. If I can study, make myself prepared, I will devote the rest of my days to every act of restoration."

From the first time she was hospitalized for depression, Diana remembers the shame and guilt she felt for the mess she was in. Her doctor told her that she was like a soldier who had been sent into battle without any training. "There are men who are armed and trained for war. You walked into a war with no ammunition. You hold your head up. You will win a war you weren't prepared to fight."

Ce

GOD USED BOTH OF DIANA'S HOSPITAL VISITS to speak hope to her spirit. The second visit He used to put her heart back together again. "Everything had been stolen from my life," Diana said. "But God began to heal me."

Diana applied for a scholarship to return to school, and the day after she was released from the hospital, she received a full scholarship to college.

Lee moved Savannah away, keeping her isolated from Diana for almost two years. Listening slack-jawed to her story as we sat on the rusted old freezer that day, I heard her prayers for a reconnection with her first daughter. To the day of this writing, Diana has yet to be able to find her daughter's address or have access to her phone number. She has immersed herself in raising Colton, her grandson, and caring for Mariah while making good on her promises to God.

"Bonnie, I've found my destiny in the valley. In the darkness I've found the capacity in Christ to see beyond where I am," Diana told me. "When I asked God how I could survive this, He spoke to my heart to look beyond it…to look beyond the circumstances and into where Savannah is.

"When I breathe, I breathe in God. God is all that has kept this from becoming a cancer to my soul."

Diana said she wears the garment of grace. "Because I pick up those robes of grace every day, I am able to see Savannah as a child. I am able to see beyond where she is and see her as my baby, child, hurting girl, struggling woman—manipulated, caught, and now in a life that has separated us. If I were not able to extend this grace, Savannah's life would be destroyed. If I were not able to forgive her, to forgive myself, she would have nowhere to go. She was victimized. Grace is the only salvation for any of us."

After Savannah had been taken away, Diana's prayer was to speak with her beloved daughter again. Almost two years had gone by without any contact. One day, Savannah called Mariah to tell her she had given birth to a baby boy.

"It was terribly difficult," Diana said. "It was like my heart breaking to bits all over again. I had prayed that God would make the scales of deception fall from Savannah's eyes before a child came into their lives. Yet I knew that perhaps motherhood would connect us in a new way. And I don't want that child to suffer through a divorce. The baby is innocent." Although they haven't yet seen each other again, Diana and Savannah continue to talk every two or three weeks. Daily, Diana picks up that robe of grace and asks God to fill her heart with forgiveness and love.

Perhaps—perhaps—motherhood will reconnect a grace-robed mother with her wounded daughter. This is Diana's prayer. Savannah sends her pictures of the baby and tries to reach out as much as she is able from her situation.

"If I ever get to hug her again, I will hold her so close, so tightly, I don't know if I'll ever be able to let her go," Diana admits.

DIANA'S ACADEMIC WORK IS ANOTHER WAY she's kept her promises to God. She is finishing her bachelor's degree in social work, and then she will start right away into the master's degree program. Diana has made the dean's list three years in a row, has been given the Outstanding Student Award, and has been inducted into both the Phi Theta Kappa and the Phi Kappa Phi societies.

Diana's heart burns with desire to speak hope to others who have messy lives, and to show the love of Christ to a hurting world.

"But the legacy and heritage I'm leaving to my girls cannot be written on a paper or earned in a degree," she told me. "I placed my blessing on Savannah and Mariah when they were babies. It's their destiny to know the Lord, to be filled with His presence."

Diana loves this quote by Johann Wolfgang von Goethe: "Miracle is faith's favorite child." Diana proclaims her Savannah to be the child of her faith in what God can do in the future.

"I believe that I have found my life's purpose, my destiny, in the valley. I have asked God that, if He will allow me to survive this, He would anoint me with His grace and that others would see Him in my face," Diana said. "If His Son could suffer such profound agony for me, then I can do this. I can get beyond this and live for God. On the other side of this, I know that there will be such joy that I will not be able to contain it. Every day I get out of bed with that promise in my heart."

For now, Diana describes herself as living in a "pregnant pause." Her master's degree will come next, and perhaps a book. She is ready to walk into the season of ministry God is preparing for her. I cannot help but believe that the work of this well-seasoned heart of grace will be profound and far-reaching.

Diana told me that her life is like the story of the turtle that ends up on top of a fencepost. "There's no way the turtle could ever have climbed onto that fencepost. Somebody, something, some circumstance, had to land that turtle there. I'm like that turtle. God has put me on the fencepost, and I'm there for a reason. With my robes of grace, I can see beyond where I am up on this post. I know the story isn't over. And the end will be awesome. So for now, I'm just staying on this fencepost. I trust God to take it from here."

The Lord *raises the poor up from the dust, and he lifts the needy from the ashes...There is no one holy like the* LORD. *There is no God but you; there is no Rock like our God.*

1 SAMUEL 2:8,2

Chapter Nine

GOD HEARD

Hannah

HANNAH'S NAME IS INTERPRETED *from the Hebrew as "grace."*
Yet reading her story in 1 Samuel, I find a woman who was
shown little grace by those around her.

Hannah was one of the two wives of a man named
Elkanah. The practice of polygamy was commonplace, yet it
was never approved by God. When God came into the world in
the form of His Son, He addressed marriage and adultery quite
clearly. He put to rest any notion that He smiled upon any
vows other than the ones He originally designed for one man
and one woman in the Garden.

Immediately, my sympathies lie with Hannah in the
obvious challenges of dealing with the other wife, Peninnah.
Hannah's grief was continually deepened because Peninnah
had children and Hannah was barren. Of course, Hannah
lived long before infertility clinics, in vitro fertilization, and
adoption procedures were available for women who longed to
have children. She turned her pleas for motherhood completely
over to God in prayer.

Peninnah must have been a tough, cruel woman, for Hannah was so tormented by her taunting that she would fall into deep depression, crying and unable to eat. Year after year this continued. "Don't I mean more to you than ten sons?" Elkanah would ask her. But still she grieved.

Then there came a breaking point, on one particular trip to Shiloh. After the family had been together for their meal, Hannah got up and went to pray to the Lord. Eli the priest was sitting on a chair near the entrance of the Lord's house. Hannah cried out to the Lord and perhaps made a promise to Him for the first time. If God would give her a son, she would give him back to the Lord to be a servant all of his life.

Eli thought she was drunk, for as she prayed, only her lips were moving. When he asked her to leave and accused her of drinking wine, she told him of her deep trouble, her broken heart, and of her prayers to God for relief.

The words of Eli must have carried a measure of comfort that Hannah had not yet known. For when he spoke, "Go! I wish you well. May the God of Israel give you what you asked of him," Hannah believed him, put away her sadness, and was willing to eat again.

Early the next day, the family traveled home to Ramah. The Bible says that God remembered Hannah's words and promises, and upon their return, Elkanah and Hannah conceived a son whom they named Samuel. His name is interpreted "God heard."

Hannah kept her covenant to the Lord. She nursed her son and kept him at home until he was able to eat. Then she returned with Samuel to Shiloh and the house of the Lord where she gave Samuel into Eli's care. Her words have been sung about, and written or carved on many a baby's picture frame ever since:

> *I prayed for this child, and the LORD answered my prayer and gave him to me. Now I give him back to the LORD. He will belong to the LORD all his life.*

Hannah's story serves as a reminder that we are never alone. Even in a crowd, we can feel shut out and forgotten. When everyone around us seems to have something we also desire...a spouse, a child, a job, a family, a friendship, health...God through Christ stands there with us. No matter how dire the situation, we must keep knocking at the door until it is opened. The mercies of the Lord are truly new every morning. Here is how Hannah might have seen things...

I FELT SO ALONE. SO TERRIBLY ALONE. Even though I was married, I felt alone. I prayed for years. Praying was my way of surviving.

It was hard enough that my husband, Elkanah, had chosen for himself two wives. I loved Elkanah with all of my heart, and I hoped I would be pleasing enough to him to fill his life with all the happiness a woman can give a man. To be fair, I was unable to fill Elkanah's life with sons and daughters. Perhaps that is why he brought Peninnah into our lives. She was as fertile as the day is long. From her womb, Elkanah had many sons and daughters, while I remained childless.

Without children, how can a woman be complete? My barren womb set me apart. Surrounded by Peninnah's children and a loving husband, still I ached with loneliness—my empty arms longed to hold a child of my own.

My husband loved me deeply and offered special blessings to me when we would go to Shiloh to give our sacrifices to the Lord All-Powerful. To Peninnah, Elkanah would give meat for her and her children. But to me, Elkanah would give an extra amount of meat to show his affection, and because he knew that God had kept me from having children. It was on our yearly journey to Shiloh that Peninnah would drive home the fact that I was barren. She was merciless with her teasing; she embarrassed me in front of others.

I was never one to fight her. Most of the time I could dismiss her unkind words. But in Shiloh, where I knew I would find myself in the Lord's house, begging Him again for mercy, my childless circumstances seemed more painful than ever. I retreated and became very depressed.

I made the journeys to Shiloh with our family year after year, praying that God would see my sadness and come to my aid. Elkanah thought I was too easily upset. He never understood how Peninnah's teasing drove me to despair. Only a woman can torment another woman so. At last, I completely lost my appetite. The thought of eating just didn't seem worth it. I began to lose weight, which worried Elkanah. He could not understand and wondered why his love was not enough for me. He asked me, was his love not worth far more than even the love of ten sons?

I could have asked him the same question. Was my love not enough, or did he not require Peninnah to provide him with a family? It wasn't that I didn't appreciate my husband. I suppose I just could not make my peace with God and my passion to be a mother. My loneliness continued to increase as time went on, and I felt more than ever estranged from everyone. One year, on our journey to Shiloh, I left the family to go and pray to Yahweh God once more. This time, not having eaten anything, weak and weary to my bones, I cried out to God with a promise I had never dared pray. I asked Him to remember me, to see my sadness, and I promised the Lord that if He would give me a son, I would give him back to the Lord to be a holy man.

I don't know how long I prayed. It must have been a long time. I do recall sitting by the entrance of the Lord's house, my eyes closed, only able to move my lips, with no sound coming from me. My prayers would not stop.

Eli the priest saw me and was confused by my behavior. He accused me of being drunk and told me to put away my wine. Drunk? Oh no! I told him that, if anything, I was drunk with prayers and pleading over my condition—delirious from battling with Peninnah and crying out to God.

I begged the Lord for a son and promised I would never hold the child too tightly, never let the child take the place of my love for my God, and that I would raise that son to be a sinless man.

Eli listened to me, saw my heart, and said to me he wished me well. He prayed that the God of Israel would grant me all I had asked of Him. In his kindness my spirit found comfort. I felt at peace. I went back to my family. The next day, with renewed peace I rose and worshiped the Lord for His great mercy. I ate a meal, and it tasted good! We journeyed home, and there was a calm, sweet, peace in my soul.

The next tears I cried were ones of joy—when my first son was born! Because the Lord Almighty did hear me, I named this son Samuel, "God heard." Elkanah was so proud and so happy to become a father to this son born of our union, our love, and God's faithfulness. I nursed Samuel until he was strong enough to eat solid food.

When he was still a young boy, I made the trip back to Shiloh, where I gave my precious son to Eli so he could raise him and teach him the ways of the Lord. Impossible, you say! How could I give up the son I had prayed for? But I had made a promise to the Lord, and He to me.

I had peace knowing that God had great plans for my Samuel. So I visited him, loved him through the years, and watched with wonder at how he grew to be a great man of God. Under the care of Eli, and full of the Spirit of the Lord, Samuel grew to be a prophet, and news of my son spread throughout Israel.

And God continued to show favor to me and to Elkanah. To honor my obedience, he opened my body to conceive again and again. I became the mother of three more sons and two daughters! From a barren womb, from an impossible situation, God used a willing heart to bring mighty things.

Giving God Control

God did not give us a spirit of timidity (of cowardice, of craven and cringing and fawning fear), but [He has given us a spirit] of power and of love…

2 TIMOTHY 1:7 (AMP)

Chapter Ten

BATTLING FEAR, REMEMBERING TO BREATHE

Bonnie's Story

MY PRECIOUS MOM LIVES IN FEAR that one of her three children (all 40 and over) will die a tragic early death. When we were teenagers, if she didn't hear from us after a date or a trip, she assumed we were "in a ditch." It never seemed to dawn on Mom that we might be tied up in traffic! Even now, when we're late for a family event, Mom is certain we'll end up on the nightly news report: abducted, pillaged, mugged, or something worse.

Now that I have children, I'll admit to the adrenaline rush that floods through me if either Courtney or Graham is unaccounted for. When Graham was a toddler, he loved to find a circular clothes rack in a department store and sit in the center of it, then enjoy the mania that ensued when I couldn't find him. I'd call his name, threaten to beat his bootie, page him over the store speakers—nothing would bring him out of hiding until he'd hear me crying. After hugging him with joy, I could never quite bring myself to do the "beating" part.

When Courtney got her driver's license, I realized my fight against the "ditches" was going to be a tough one. She's very responsible and not a risk-taker, but…what about those idiot drivers who might get in her way? Each morning, I pray for a legion of car angels to surround her Saturn—the little car we call "Goldie." All the ditch images begin to crop up in my mind, but I refuse to live with a knot in my stomach. And I thank God when I hear "Goldie" pull in at night.

The only time I ever really feel at peace is when it's late at night and everyone is in their bed, safe and asleep!

Giving over my thoughts to an imagined tragedy is a terrible way to rob myself of the present. When the fears begin to creep into my mind, I fight back with the messages of faith I know to be true. "Do not be afraid" is spoken to the human race in the Bible 365 times, one time for each day of the year. The message comes from God, from angels, from Jesus and the words of His followers. The good Lord must have known that we humans would need to be reminded to take our eyes off of the whirlwind of events that distract our hearts, and be reminded to remember that He is in control. Do not freak out! God has the final say. He knows the end of each of our stories and each moment that makes up the tapestry of our lives. Our names are written in His private journal.

We humans can easily panic when the waves of fear threaten to capsize our lives. When Jesus was awakened by His terrified disciples on their boat during a rough storm, He asked, "Why are you so fearful? Where is your faith, your trust, your confidence in Me—in My veracity and My integrity?" Then He calmed the angry waves.

Ҩҽҽ

ON THE OTHER HAND, HEALTHY FEAR is a good thing. Being afraid of being careless…of being too quick to speak in anger or acting out of pride, jealousy, self-indulgence—fear can be a wonderfully helpful instinct. From childhood, we learn how not to play in the street for fear that we will be killed, not to touch hot objects like irons and burners on stoves; we learn to avoid substances that will harm our bodies or draw us into addictions, and hopefully, to have a hearty fear of ruinous relationships.

And a productive, awe-struck, grateful fear of God—that He truly is God and we are not, that He knows best the paths our lives should take and will be there to see us through this life—that is the best of all flavors of fear.

In looking at the lives of many men and women of the Bible, the fear of God can be seen giving them tremendous strength. It was a fearful trust of God that led Noah to build an ark in a world that had never seen a drop of rain! Abraham had the incredible courage, from fearing God, to take his son Isaac and lay him on an altar as a sacrifice as God asked him to do. These acts of fear-filled trust continue to utterly confound us.

In the New Testament, a man named Cornelius was used to change the face of Christianity because "he and all the other people who lived in his house feared and worshiped the true God." Cornelius was an officer in the Roman army, one who would normally have been a target of hatred from the Jews. Yet because of his fearful respect of God, he was used to show Peter that Jesus had come for more people than just the Jews. Jesus had come to save anyone who would love, follow, and fearfully engage in a relationship with God. What a rich flavor of fear Cornelius experienced!

⟡

C.S. LEWIS WRITES THAT THE FEELING OF FEAR is in itself no place of shame. Yet allowing fear to transform us into cowards is a tragedy. This kind of fear turns the backbone of faith to jelly. It promises to protect the heart by refusing to be humble and open to change. It turns a deaf ear to the call of God. Terrified of being wrong, this kind of fear resists asking for forgiveness or allowing a response of transparent repentance.

This flavor of fear is fatal.

Protective fear only guards the status quo and leaves no room for growth, tenderness, compassion, or grace. In the name of cowardly fear, millions of people have suffered the deaths of friendships, have suffered broken hearts, have endured hard-lined legalistic theology that drives countless people away from God, have been tortured, and have died.

Fear began in the Garden of Eden when Adam and Eve hid from God after their disobedience, having eaten from the one tree they were asked to avoid like the plague. Fear entered the world and opened Pandora's box and plague upon plague of fear followed.

Fear of being wrong quenches the flames of forgiving grace and drives the nails into the hands and feet of Jesus to make them bleed. And yet Jesus died, taking on Himself all the flavors of fear that would tear at our hearts, in order to give us freedom from fear. Perfect love in Christ banishes fear, but we must be awake to the crafty packaging with which the enemy wraps its nastier flavors. After all, many a fearful heart has simply given up on God.

Fear invades like a cancer when death comes upon a loved one, unexpectedly, untimely, without mercy.

Fear creeps in and takes up residence in hearts that long for love, hearts that are broken from betrayal; in its presence prayers can seem lost somewhere in time, unheard or unanswered by God.

Fear whispers into the ears of clergymen, teachers, businessmen—to be protective, to guard the status quo...to become bigger and better and more powerful in an attempt to be secure in an insecure world.

Fear poisons the lifeblood of faith when churches turn their backs on the unsavory people they cannot understand: the divorced, the single parents, the addicts, the homosexuals, the prostitutes—the poorly clothed, disheveled, messy ones who are in the most earnest need of a kind word, a touch, a brief eye-to-eye contact.

We must not allow these flavors of fear to keep us from reaching out—for help and to help others.

Fear of being barren caused Abraham's wife Sarah to send her maidservant in to her husband to conceive an illegitimate child. And Abraham's fear for his life caused him to lie about Sarah's being his wife, calling her his sister when confronted by the Egyptians. Fear ran through the veins of Aaron—after leading the Israelites from Egypt into the desert, seeing the parting of the Red Sea, being fed from heaven by God, still this man of God allowed the Hebrews to build a golden calf to worship.

Fear nipped at the heels of even Peter, who, upon Jesus' arrest, lied about knowing his Lord three times.

Christ loved Peter in spite of his messy profession of faith, his insistence that he would never deny Jesus. Christ knew that Peter was weak, human—that he would fear while stepping out of the boat and attempting to walk on the waters to meet Jesus. Christ knew that Peter would fall asleep when asked to stay awake to pray.

Astoundingly human—meaning well in his heart but failing at every turn—Peter was understood by Jesus in all of his brokenness, weakness, and fear. In Matthew 16:17-19, we read Jesus' words to Peter: "My Father in heaven showed you who I am. So I tell you...on this rock I will build my church, and the power of death will not be able to defeat it. I will give you the keys of the kingdom of heaven." When Peter insisted on his unfailing loyalty, Christ did not shame him but replied, "Simon, Simon, Satan has asked to test all of you as a farmer sifts his wheat. I have prayed that you will not lose your faith! Help your brothers be stronger when you come back to me" (Luke 22:31-32).

Our human, messy fears are no surprise to God.

> *Fear of failure,*
> *Fear of being hurt,*
> *Fear of the unknown,*
> *Fear of being wrong,*
> *Fear of coming clean,*
> *Fear of yesterday's pain, today's mountain,*
> *tomorrow's future,*
> *All of these fears were abolished on the cross.*
> *These are human fears.*
> *They are part of us.*

Carried inside and left to fester, these fears can keep us from the loving release of God's grace. But fear loses its power when it's brought out of hiding. The paralyzing trance is broken when we are led into the light.

Do not be afraid. Each day, 365 times a year, God speaks courage in Christ, courage to replace your fears. Do not be afraid to take the hidden fears that separate you from the peace of Jesus and lay them at His feet.

***

WHENEVER I AM FEARFUL, I HAVE TO remember to slow down and take deep breaths. To remember my faith. To remember to breathe.

As a child, growing up in the buckle of the Bible Belt in Nashville, I recall many times when life slowed down, at least on Sundays. Contrary to popular belief, fueled by the characters of the television show *Hee Haw* and by many incorrect portrayals of life below the Mason-Dixon line, we Southerners do wear shoes, and we run the rat race well, right alongside our northern, western, and eastern neighbors. But there was a brief time, I remember, when malls, gas stations, and grocery stores would put out the "Closed" sign on the first day of the week. If we didn't have enough of any particular thing, we just did without until Monday rolled around.

This was the atmosphere in a time before cell phones, fax machines, and ATM huts. It was a time when banks shut their doors on Friday and there was no hope of getting cash until the next workweek. Weekends were truly weekends—time for family, friends, and church—a time to breathe. Life simply moved into a graceful holding pattern for a few days before the world kicked into high gear once more.

It's almost impossible to imagine the world slowing down now for any reason. Even on Christmas Day there are stores open, and if you stop for gasoline at many a convenience store, a poor, tired face will look back at you and say, "Yeah...I have to work today at least until 3 or 4..." Time is no longer sacred.

Yet even God Himself rested on the seventh day after His whirlwind of creating! In the top ten commandments, those given for the good health and sanity of His people, He included "Keep the Sabbath Day holy." God asked His people to set apart one day each week—to drink from, to absorb, and to breathe in the sanctity of life.

I'm guilty. Guilty to the core in my own life of failing to observe the precious treasure of a Sabbath rest. And when I get into my "works" mode, I find myself running on fumes, exhausted and depressed. I set myself up for failure every time I allow my schedule to get out of control, or allow my "doing" to take a front seat to my "being." When I put God first, my emotions stay in balance and my mind is more whole. When I turn into "the little engine that could" and think I can do everything, I might as well call the mental hospital and book a room.

My guilt about my heavy schedule has resulted in a recurring, fear-filled dream. In my dream, I am driving a car downhill, quickly gaining speed and losing control. Usually I am careening toward something I cannot see, or heading toward a drop off at the end of the road. As I hurtle downward, I am leaning back in the driver's seat, pressing with all of my might on the brakes of the car with both of my feet. Determined to stop the car, I fight panic, but I'm helpless to change my collision course. I'm never clear as to where the car is headed. I have no specific deadline, person, or event at this crash site. I just want the car to stop! And the nightmarish part of the dream is that no matter what I do to slow the car down, nothing works. The brakes are unconditionally ineffective. The inevitable catastrophe looms closer and closer... The car is out of control, it picks up speed, it moves faster and faster...

I wake from this nightmare fearful, in a cold sweat. The surreal experience has once again ended before impact. Yet this dream reveals, once more, one of the demons I battle. I am once more fully engaged in overload. My fears of caving in appear in my subconscious, warning me in the night, illuminating my heart.

I am afraid.

Too much is going on.

I cannot breathe.

Recently, as I was driving I passed a billboard on the highway that promised in bold, black type "24/7/365—Call Us Anytime!" As I passed the sign I felt the urge to stand on the brakes of my car. My pulse quickened, and I felt a sudden rush of anxiety. The intense pace of our lives is out of control, like the car in my dreams that refuses to come to a halt.

The challenge of living in this 24/7 cultural environment is to make "being alone" and "being still" as important as the endless stream of church gatherings, charity work, school activities, and social events. For it is not until we stop, or are forced to stop by a physical or emotional collapse, that we are able to hear and enjoy and be delighted in our God.

As Jesus walked this earth, He became tired and weary. He understands the pressures of life because He lived a life here. He urges me to let go, give out, and find rest in Him. He invites us, "Come to Me, all you who labor and are heavy-laden *and* overburdened, and I will cause you to rest. [I will ease and relieve and refresh your souls.] Take My yoke upon and learn of Me, for I am gentle (meek) and humble (lowly) in heart, and you will find rest (relief and ease and refreshment and recreation and blessed quiet) for your souls."

It is up to each of us to learn from the example of God on this Earth. Jesus could not earn or work for acceptance from His Father God. He walked in full knowledge that God's love was His. He did not apologize for needing time to be still; He simply took it as a necessity for equipping Himself to give to the world.

Messy situations, messy lives, and hurting souls have to stop and be rearranged, put back together, and strengthened again. When we work too hard and rush around too quickly, we find only emptiness and disappointment. Our messy, fearful lives require us to catch our breath. As you run the race, don't be afraid to take time out to rest in the arms of God.

Remember to breathe.

In the time of your life—live. That time is short and it doesn't return again. It is slipping away while I write this and while you read it, and the monosyllable of the clock is loss, loss, loss unless you devote your heart to its opposition.

TENNESSEE WILLIAMS

Chapter Eleven

FEAR-FILLED TRUST
Four Women's Stories

NOTHING HAS DRIVEN HOME TO ME the incredible value of each day as much as watching several of my close friends go through breast cancer surgery and reconstructive surgery. It's been an experience of agony for each courageous woman and her family. These are women in the prime of their lives—active, astoundingly beautiful, optimistic, with inner and outer beauty that turns the head of everyone in a room that they enter.

Sue, my friend, a talented writer (and soon to be honored by a shrine I am planning to build on my property, fully equipped with outdoor lighting and a bubbling fountain!), is a more-than-20-year survivor of this dreaded disease. The title of her first book, *I'm Alive and the Doctor Is Dead,* tells it all. With great spirit and a wicked sense of humor, she's beaten the odds. After outliving a grim prognosis, she's now speaking all over the country and has authored many popular books.

I especially love her theory on chocolate. In her flyaway-blonde-hair-short-skirted way, Sue has managed to get major medical organizations to take notice of her passionate belief that a large daily intake of chocolate can keep cancer at bay. Her pocket, purse, or luggage contains an endless assortment of Hershey's or other choice chocolate options. Sue's personal daily chocolate vitamin is your basic milk-chocolate brand—anything that fires you up. Dark chocolate is not quite as medicinal...but is allowed (though Sue won't use it!).

My friend Marlei, a young mother of three, is smart, humble, and has a heart full of grace. She's worked all over the country with top recording artists and has that rare ability to take the most difficult public-relations scenarios and pull them together without a hitch. Marlei is also drop-dead gorgeous; she reminds me of Grace Kelly—blonde, tiny, beautiful skin...you want to hate her, but she's too wonderful to even try.

After Marlei was diagnosed with stage-four breast cancer, she went through the worst and came back. She never whined or complained. Like Sue, she looked the monster in the face, and did each next thing there was to do to fight back. She did weep with fear at times, and she reached out for help and prayers. Marlei found courage in her faith. After her last chemo treatments were completed, she and her husband traveled to Europe with a close-knit group of friends for a celebration. Defeat is not in her vocabulary. Now in full recovery, she's going on with her life as bravely as ever.

MY WORK—SINGING IN THE RECORDING-STUDIO industry here in Nashville—has allowed me to become good friends with many other singers. Over the years and the shared hours in the studio, they've woven threads of strength and wit into the tapestry of my life. On the soprano microphone (where I've spent more hours than I can count) I am often privileged to be able to sing, laugh, and pray with a beautiful woman, Mary, who sings like an angel. We all want to grow up and sound like Mary, who blushes and waves her arms to push us away when we compliment her on the notes she reaches with perfection, light as air, the ones higher than dogs can hear.

Mary's battle with breast cancer began a few months after her father died. This woman of faith and courage soon plunged into the world of surgeries and treatments and reconstruction and other horrors. Mary was able to laugh and find moments of humor in her situation, which I find amazing. In the midst of additional reconstructive surgery, she also is caring for her mother, who has been diagnosed with Lou Gehrig's disease. Her faith in the risen Christ—in all that Jesus came to suffer for and give to her for times such as these—fuels the steady flame of calm hope in her heart.

My friend Patty Sue is a walking testament to the sense of humor God can sustain in someone diagnosed with cancer. When Patty Sue found out that she was going to have radiation and chemotherapy—the whole nine yards—she called those closest to her for prayer. Then she matter-of-factly made plans about what to do with her life, and what to do without her thick, dark brown, stunning, nearly waist-length head of hair. Just the thought of Patty Sue without her trademark braid down her back was impossible!

However, with total class she did everything she could do to be the likeness of Jesus in her pain. What the enemy of this world means to use to destroy, the people of God can use to His glory. Patty found a place where she could donate her hair to be used to make wigs for children who had lost their hair from disease or cancer treatment. Her husband shaved his head, and her best friend at work vowed to do the same until Patty stopped her.

On Christmas Eve, Patty celebrated the last of her chemotherapy sessions. She and her husband, Wayne, invited Brent and me to go with them and a few other friends on a limousine ride to see the Christmas lights around town. When we showed up, Patty Sue was standing there, dressed to the max, bald as a baby, wearing a long Santa Claus cap that would flop from side to side on her head when she pushed the right button.

Thankful to God for His grace, we had a fantastic night eating dinner at a restaurant, where Patty would sit quietly smiling, then without warning would turn the flopping hat on to the delight of all around us. Alternately, she would remove the Santa cap and put on a wreath made of Christmas lights and a garland. She would giggle like a kid who had stolen the cookies from the cookie jar when she caused someone to stop and stare. I could see the spirit and humor of Jesus looking out from her eyes, the gift of laughter in the midst of pain.

I HAVE WITNESSED REMARKABLE STRENGTH and bravery through the example of these women. Loss of hair, body parts, appetite, and energy has not robbed them of their determination to protect their lives and children and relationship with their husbands. Each one has faced the monster down and has a section of cheering, admiring fans praying for them as they begin a new season in their lives. Each one has a faith that has sustained them in the midst of ridiculous odds, outrageous, inhumane treatments, and vicious attacks on their self-esteem.

When I think of the lovely face of each one of these survivors, I stand humbled at their valor. I'm a wimp! I had a near miss with a suspicious lump in my breast years ago, and how quickly I caved in to fear, cried, and trembled through the three-month checkups.

Each woman I have written of here has offered those around her the gift of seeing her live out her trust and faith in the work Jesus came into this world to do for us all. And each of these women has known the value of cherishing each moment of life. They have known the value of each day, and they continue to make the most of their time.

Clee

I LOVE WATCHING PEOPLE AT AN AIRPORT. Traveling has long been a part of my life, and in spite of my early years of throwing up on every car ride, God has put me in a profession that requires lots of travel. (His sense of humor never ceases to amaze me.) Thankfully, the nausea has morphed into the need to sleep, but I also enjoy watching the human dramas that unfold in airport terminals.

The most poignant scene I can remember was of a precious older woman in a wheelchair complete with an oxygen tank. She was brought up to our gate after her original flight had been canceled. I use the word "up" because she was literally wheeled up from many floors below the boarding area. She'd been visiting her family in California and was returning to her home in Florida. Somehow, her flight had been delayed and then canceled. She was taken off the original plane and put near an elevator to wait for a "red coat" representative from the airline to escort her to the next gate. Well, amid the confusion of the Atlanta airport (a nightmarish "interlude" for frequent travelers), the "red coat" never showed up. This poor lady was finally discovered next to a secluded elevator in the guts of the airport, sitting scared and alone in her wheelchair. She was quickly taken by a nervous agent and parked by the gate in the main terminal so as not to be misplaced again.

Airline representatives were scurrying around with furrowed brows, trying to calm the woman and most likely fearing she might keel over right then and there. Meanwhile, the woman loudly voiced her terrible experience to all of us sitting around her. We shook our heads and tried to be sympathetic. I couldn't resist my best mother-style glance of disapproval at the airline representatives who had left this woman unattended, sucking on her oxygen mask in the black hole of the airport.

In her thick New York accent, she repeated over and over, "All I'm trying to do is go home. They've stolen my Thursday. They've stolen my Thursday." It struck me to the heart. There wasn't a hint of petulance in her tone or attitude. Yet she repeated this phrase over and over, like a child whose most prized stuffed animal had vanished.

It made me think. At her age, this woman truly understood that time is precious and irretrievable. It drips away like sand in an hourglass. Obviously this dear lady must have valued every single Thursday she had left in this world. Sitting for hours trapped by airline schedules that go awry, she felt robbed of a portion of her life.

Stopping to absorb the poignancy of her fear, taking in her shaking hands and her sad face, I realized once again how sacred and precious this gift of life is.

How many times do I miss a special moment in my eagerness to get to the next place? I remember a friend of mine who'd survived a near fatal illness, once shouted "I'm here! I'm alive and in this chair! This is the best day of my life!"

With all the chaos, tumult, and rushed schedules that life holds, it is still a miracle how we live and breathe and have a chance to leave something meaningful behind us. I see evidence of God's love in this gift called life. The gift of being— just being wherever we are called by God to be that particular day—is simple, holy, and irreplaceable.

I want to know the passion for life these women know. I want to fight for each day, to guard it and see its value. I want to wake up each morning and just say,

Thank You, Lord, for another chance to live.

In whatever this day may bring
may I have the manna of grace
to see the miracle that I have another day—
another chance to reach out, forgive, learn,
laugh, dance, or just sit and be...

Another chance to be grateful for life,
and for my Thursdays...
and for all the days in between.

God never intended for me to work hard, I can see that now. My true calling in life is to live unencumbered and follow the fleeting impulses of my heart and take a nap around 2 P.M.

GARRISON KEILLOR,
in *Time* magazine

Chapter Twelve

TOO BUSY TO BE
Martha

CHRIST SPOKE BEAUTIFULLY TO THE "WORKS" *mentality in the story of His friendship with Mary and Martha, the sisters of one of His best friends, Lazarus. He would often visit them—their home seemed to be a place where Jesus could relax and enjoy their laughter and affection. It was a space for Him to regroup and simply "be." Mary was comfortable simply being. Her sister Martha was a doer.*

I AM MARTHA, THE SISTER OF Mary and Lazarus. Jesus loved us so, and He would always make time to visit our home when He was passing through our village. Of course, around here we have an open-door policy. There is always some type of festivity going on around here most any time of the day or night. I'm good at organizing. I love cooking and being in charge of events, gatherings, and arrangements for those I am closest to. I'm a servant by heart and nature. It's my gift.

If you'll excuse my saying so, unlike my sister Mary, who is content with doing as little as possible, I have to be occupied with a project to feel useful. Jesus knew this about me and loved me anyway. One day in particular, I was busy getting food ready for Him, and Mary was not lifting a finger to help! She was just sitting at the feet of Jesus. They were talking and laughing...relaxing, I guess. Perhaps I was a bit jealous, and more than a little bit peeved at my sister's selfish laziness. So I asked Jesus if it didn't bother Him to see that Mary was leaving me to do all the preparation. Actually, I told Him to tell her to do her part, if you can believe my audacity!

He smiled at me, sighed for a moment, and then took my hand in His and said, "Martha, you are so anxious, so troubled, so busy. You work so hard on too many things. Maybe you could learn from Mary the great lesson of just being. Life isn't really that complicated. And it goes by so quickly. There is precious little time for the best moments. Don't miss them."

He used my anxiety to teach me about the holiness of life. How each new day brings new things to be lived, to be breathed in. We didn't have Him long enough here on this Earth. He needed a safe place to relax, a safe place to enjoy without the pressures that followed Him everywhere He went. My eyes fill with tears of gratitude when I realize that our home was such a place for Him. So very many times I wish I had spent less time cooking and more time with Mary at His feet...simply being together with Him, our most precious Lord and friend. But then He also taught me not to regret or dwell on things I cannot change.

One thing is certain. When I get to heaven, whether He likes it or not, I'm going to cook Him the best meal He's ever had. It may take me all of eternity to prepare it. I will most certainly take my time and enjoy it. And when He comes to my house again, I'll delight in His presence like never before.

ALL HUMAN BEINGS NEED GREAT FRIENDS—*true-blue companions who are safe, fun, and who offer deep wells of refreshment. Jesus was no exception to this. We all need companions who give back to us as we give to them. The "takers" in life are always there and are always willing to suck the life out of us if we allow them. The "givers" are few and far between. These relationships are precious, priceless places—each an oasis where we can go and let ourselves be known inside and out, where we can feel accepted, loved, and treasured.*

Martha, Mary, and their brother, Lazarus, were three of Jesus' closest and most beloved friends. When Lazarus died, Jesus wept with the family, even knowing that He would soon bring His friend back to life. Jesus cried because He knew that we live in a world where best friends weren't meant to die. Human tears from God in Christ…suffering shared…as well as laughter and joy.

Martha and Mary's home was a safe haven for Christ. He visited them often and was nurtured by their companionship. Unfortunately, I relate most to Martha, the frantic doer. I love the story of how Jesus spoke truth into her life about lightening up a bit, encouraged her to relax. It was God speaking into her heart that this world was made first as a garden…tilling the ground is necessary, but what good does it do if one does not stop long enough to see the beautiful results?

Loved—In Spite of the Mess

The devil never rejoices more than when he robs a servant of God of his peace of heart.

FRANCIS OF ASSISI

Chapter Thirteen

FACES OF HOPELESSNESS

Bonnie's Story

ERRING ON THE SIDE OF BRUTAL HONESTY, I've decided to
start this part of the book by opening a vein. It's taken me far
too long to find the courage to begin this chapter. Why?
Because I find my own heart battling hard against waves of
hopelessness and despair.

I wish I could write that I never wrestle before God with
depression and questions that plague me in the night, but
that would be a lie. It was much less disturbing to write
about being too busy, being tired, being distracted, being
worn-out. Now, I'm going to come clean at a more intimate
level. God forbid that anyone pick up this book and read it
thinking that I have my "spiritual ducks" all in a row! It's difficult to admit my own weakness. My prayer is that, in being
vulnerable, I can speak hope to other hopeless ones. Trusting
in God's character, in the great redemptive love of Christ,
and in the ongoing work of the Holy Spirit gives me hope. Yet
I constantly need to remind myself of God's truths as the
world around me screams in pain and as, at certain
moments, darkness comes upon me like a raging animal.

For many years, I could attribute much of my depression and loss of hope to divorce, single parenthood, losing my ministry with First Call, and simply trying to stay alive financially, spiritually, and emotionally. In those desperate years, Christ became very real to me. God has been merciful to move my life on into a place of peace. Now I am in a new marriage, and a new season of beauty surrounds me—but I must confess that my soul still confronts depression and despair. Life has its way of bringing me to my knees, and I have begun to accept this without shame, as a human condition that Jesus Himself understands.

I've talked and written to enough others to know that this war we fight—against the powers and principalities, against the prince of this world of death—is a common experience of many people. I have a tendency to look at those around me, especially at church, and think, "If only I were as 'together' as that person, I wouldn't be such a recovering basket case."

As Charles Schulz's Charlie Brown put it so perfectly, "Sometimes I lie awake at night and ask, 'Where did I go wrong?' Then I hear, 'This is going to take more than one night.'"

What causes us to lose hope? There is nothing quite so deafening as the silence of lost dreams, lost will, the emptiness of defeat.

> *Divorce,*
> *Death,*
> *Loss of friendships,*
> *Angry or thoughtless words from family,*
> *Lack of self-esteem,*
> *Disappointment by a beloved one,*
> *Betrayal,*
> *Debt,*

Seemingly unanswered prayer,
Loneliness,
Legalism,
Condemnation,
Addictions.

So many human conditions can lead one to depression or hopelessness! These feelings are human, and unfortunately they grow normally from our fragile humanity.

But thank God that His love is completely and utterly abnormal. There is nothing normal about a God who would come to Earth and live as one of us. There is nothing about God's love that is normal. He loves people who turn their backs on Him, saints and sinners alike. Through His crazy love, by His taking on flesh, blood, bone, and skin, He redeems our humanness and makes it holy. This irrational reversal brings redemption for us humans, the ones He made in His likeness in the first place. After we had chosen to defy His wild love in the Garden, God decided upon an unheard of display of love to restore His creation. It's an insane love story—this dance between us and our God.

○○○

NOW BEFORE YOU THROW THIS BOOK across the room, thinking that there is no way for you to find such love, please examine one of the wilder reasons that you and I have to hope beyond our hopelessness. Consider this—many of the great, "biblical" men and women, prophets and kings, suffered these same, horrific, human feelings. We are not bad people—failures as people of faith, aberrations of nature—

when we fall at times into a place of simple grief and sad hopelessness.

Ponder for a moment the life of two men of God; one a prophet and one a king of Israel: Jonah and David.

Jonah, a prophet of God, was asked to take God's warning to the despised people of Nineveh. Instead of doing as God asked, Jonah booked a ticket in the opposite direction, to a place called Tarshish. After a storm at sea, after being cast overboard and spending three days and nights in the belly of God alone knows what kind of sea creature, Jonah found himself, prophet of the most holy God, in a pile of vomit on the shore. Jonah carried out God's call to him, convincing the Ninevites that their sins would do them in—short of an immediate about-face. Astounding as the entire story of Jonah is, what's most striking is that after the city repents and God changes His mind, showing mercy to spare the city, Jonah declares that God is indeed a powerful, loving, and compassionate God...then announces that he wants to die!

"I knew that you are a God who is kind and shows mercy. You don't become angry quickly, and you have great love. I knew you would choose not to cause harm. So now I ask you, LORD, please kill me. It is better for me to die than to live" (Jonah 4:2-3). Jonah understood the magnificence of God's love, yet he had no will to live! Such a harsh reaction from this prophet—after surviving three days and nights in the fluids of a great fish, seeing the restoration of a lost city, and tasting firsthand of God's power. Jonah was depressed!

The contemporary definition of depression is that it's anger turned in on oneself. One does not enjoy what is normally enjoyed, and begins to think of death and giving up on life. For whatever reasons, Jonah was one angry, depressed prophet. Perhaps his depression grew out of his anger that

God had given grace to such an undeserving nation. (All of us have a private list of people we feel don't "deserve" mercy.) But such a weak, human condition in this stalwart visionary of God? The book of Jonah leaves us with no knowledge of what happened to him. We do know that God did answer his angry cries with further provisions, and with patient explanation and grace.

I remember a time when I did not want to live. During this period of abdication and clinical depression, I calmly prayed my "Jonah prayer" to God: "I know that you are my Father, loving and merciful. I know that when I die, I will be with you. I will not do anything to hurt myself; I love my children and want to be strong for them. But if you wouldn't mind, Lord, would you just take me out?"

My depression turned inward—my anger about my life and how it had disappointed me led me spiraling down. In this low place, though I had no desire to blame God for my plight and more clearly than ever believed He was mercifully close to me, I simply had no will to live another day on this Earth. Jonah's words were no different than mine.

Could it be that God is not surprised by such a heart in despair? Could it be that even the men He called out for special service suffered some of the same brokenness as the rest of us?

Cee

DAVID, THE GREATEST KING OF ISRAEL, the man after God's own heart, committed adultery and murder, conceiving a child with Bathsheba, then killing her husband and marrying her. Everything about David's life had been like a faith-driven, things-go-right-against-the-giants fairy tale before these incidents. Then human nature overcame David's very human heart, and he fell flat. Fell hard. Fell into ruin.

In Psalm 38:3-6, David writes,

> *My body is sick from your punishment. Even my bones are not healthy because of my sin. My guilt has overwhelmed me; like a load it weighs me down. My sores stink and become infected because I was foolish. I am bent over and bowed down; I am sad all day long.*

And later he writes, "Record my lament; list my tears on your scroll—are they not in your record?" (Psalms 56:8 NIV).

The great King David—depressed? David longing for death? The young man who had killed a giant with slingshot and stone, whose faith had caused him to dance with abandoned passion before the Lord, was swept up in agony over his choices. Yet David knew the nature of his loving God. He had an intimate relationship with the Yahweh God he feared—and also came to in complete honesty and brokenness.

After being confronted with his sin by Nathan, the prophet sent by God to give him a wake-up call, David writes this most precious and famous song to the Lord:

> *Wash away all my guilt and make me clean again… You are the only one I have sinned against. I have done what you say is wrong…Make me hear sounds of joy and gladness; let the bones you crushed be happy again…Create in me a pure heart, God, and make my spirit right again (Psalm 51:2,4,8,10).*

God restored David to a secure place of reconciliation and forgiveness. Yet the choices David had made overshadowed him for the rest of his life, and many of his psalms speak to a very human heart that cries out—weary of life, burdened by depression, and longing for relief. When I'm asked about combating depression, I often recommend that the depressed person read from the Psalms every day. They are filled with the depths of pain, and they affirm by their very existence in the Bible that God has compassion for those who mourn and that He gives honor to them.

Oee

JOHN THE BAPTIST, ONE OF THE MOST colorful of God's prophets, appeared to be beyond human. Luke records that John was so intuitive that he actually leapt in his mother Elizabeth's womb when Mary the mother of Jesus came to visit. Even as an unborn child, this man could discern the presence of God! And so it would be appropriate that one so holy and anointed would recognize Christ in the flesh—the Messiah coming to him to be baptized, waiting His turn in line with the seeking, dirty, hopeless ones. As John realized that his work was coming full circle, he baptized Jesus and said, "He must become greater, and I must become less important" (John 3:30).

However, when John was put into prison by King Herod and awaited death in a dark, dank, and hideous cell, even this prophet of the Messiah must have had moments of doubt. How could a life so beautifully given—given in service to make the world ready for God's Son—land him in jail? In Luke 7:18-20, we see how John sent his followers to "double-check" with Jesus, to clarify once again whether or not He was truly the Messiah: "John the Baptist sent us to you with this question: 'Are you the One who is coming, or should we wait for another?'" (verse 20).

Such beauteous humanity I find in this innocent inquiry. Even John the Baptist had a chink in his armor. Even this beloved, inspired, dearest prophet had to ask, "Is this what I prophesied about? Are You really going to change things? What is going on here?"

☙

THERE ARE ECHOES OF THOSE SAME questions in the letters and e-mails I now receive, nearly 2000 years after the death and resurrection of Jesus:

> *I used to think I was fearless. Until I moved here and began to get to know myself better. I am full of fear and yearn for freedom from it. I read a verse the other day that says God's love casts out fear...that there is no fear in perfect love. Where is this Jesus I'm reading about? I want to know Him and trust Him. I want a relationship.*

☙

> *There are days when I can't even breathe...when the tears never stop, and I feel my life slipping away. It's during that time when I take every ounce of faith that I have and lift up my eyes toward heaven to allow the Lord to pick me up out of this dark pit in my life.*

☙

> *I have learned a lot through the trials of my divorce and losing my children to my ex-husband. My children lost their mom, their home, and their school (I home-schooled them) in one moment, in a biased,*

world-system courtroom. My ex had an affair and wanted to marry her and needed me out of the way. The battle continues, but I see the Lord's hand, and I await His timing for my children's deliverance.

In the prayer journal that I take on the road with me are similar pleadings for mercy and understanding:

Please pray for Audrey. She lost her two-year-old son in a drowning accident and then had brain surgery to remove a tumor. She doesn't understand how God could allow this, and being so young and newly divorced, she is now so depressed.

I am a mother of five and sometimes feel as if I'm not leading them to be strong-enough Christians. Any prayers would help.

Please pray for my sister-in-law and her two sons as they adapt to life without a daddy. Their father was killed in a carjacking in West Africa while ministering there, planting a church.

Over and over again, I also find things like this written in my prayer book: "Please pray for my peace of heart…"; "…for my family to have peace of heart"; "…for my son and my daughter to find peace of heart."

Dearest ones, we are not in this alone. The boldest men of faith battled depression, fear, doubt, and hopelessness. Can we not see that this is what binds us to Christ?

If on this day or night, if in this season of your life, you are fighting Jonah-like rage, David-like depression, John the Baptist–like doubt, I pray you will take heart by seeing that your hopelessness is nothing new to the strongest or weakest believer. Let me join with you as we find courage in Christ through seeing the humanness of His followers and by sharing in His sufferings, the sufferings of the Son of Man.

Why would Jesus be called "the Son of Man"? In *The Final Week of Jesus*, Max Lucado tells us that "this title appears eighty-two times in the New Testament. Eighty-one of which are in the Gospels. Eighty of which are directly from the lips of Jesus."

Jesus took upon Himself our humanity, calling Himself the Son of Man, so that God Himself could comprehend how hopeless even His beautiful world can be. Jesus wanted to be counted as a man among men, a man who loved so much that He willingly gave Himself to suffer every imaginable horror of hopelessness and depression on the cross. Now we have a Savior who has overcome one of the most cruel of all messy conditions—yes, even the deepest despair.

By the grace of God I am what I am, and His grace toward me was not in vain.

1 Corinthians 15:10 (NKJV)

Chapter Fourteen

MY CAPTIVITY

Garry's Story

I'LL NEVER FORGET HOW NERVOUS and intimidated I felt when I first met Garry on the set of *100 Huntley Street,* the flagship program of the Canadian Christian Television Network. As Garry walked toward Marty McCall and me, I was struck by his elegant Italianesque jacket, his impeccable manners, and his open smile. Garry has a mix of humility and grace, set off by a bit of David Niven–type charisma. From the get-go he puts you at ease and also makes you anxious to please him. He has encouraged countless Christian artists, writers, and speakers to spread the message of Christ to Canada and to the world.

With his many contacts throughout Canada and the United States, he's worn every hat—concert promoter, television producer, record distributor, fundraiser—and I've lost track of all the other plates he has spinning. When I first met him I noticed how quickly he made First Call—Marty and me—feel welcome. Here was a godly, effective messenger of God—dressed in an Armani suit. I wanted to learn more about this man.

Garry took Marty and me to lunch before our concert, and we all shared openly about our lives, feeling quite safe— and unusually intimate for strangers who had never met before. I've been a part of many "business luncheons," but this one was markedly different and nothing like I had anticipated. There was a rare, honest conversation about God's great love and the ways He had saved us all from ourselves.

Several years later, after many more visits and after wonderful rich times in which I had grown to call both Garry and his "lovely wife, Veronica" (as he refers to her) two of my dearest friends, I asked him if I could interview them about their marriage. Late one evening, I sat down with Garry and Veronica in front of a hotel fireplace to talk about his life, how he met Veronica—his "story." But as he opened his heart, I learned so much more about why Garry walks through life with such grace and with such an acute awareness of the mercy of Jesus. Saving Garry and Veronica's love story for another day, I have chosen here to share with you how Garry's horribly messy life was literally saved by Jesus.

Here is a man whose life encompasses everything I've written about in this book: feelings of unworthiness, loss, loneliness, weariness, and abandonment. Garry's life, like the lives of many others that belong in God's photo album, is one of the great miracles Jesus came to live and die for.

Clee~

GARRY'S FATHER LEFT HOME WHEN GARRY was a young child and his mother and father divorced. He watched his mother go through a series of relationships as she looked for some strength in her life, looked for a man, looked for some roots. When he was 13, Garry left his home in St. Catharine and went to Toronto to look for his father. "I was a street kid, a hobo...literally living on the streets," Garry remembers. "When I left home I had three cents and an old army pack-sack, and I just stuck my thumb out and jumped a freight train that was going up into northern Ontario. It was there that I ended up with a group of surveyors in what they called the 'bush-camp slashing gang.' I was the young kid, the 'cookie,' so I had to wash the pots and pans and peel potatoes as I traveled with the camp. I picked tobacco—just did any-thing I could."

During this time, Garry's mother remarried, and she became so wrapped up in her new life that she didn't check up on Garry at all. In turn, Garry didn't keep in touch with his mother. "I remember once, when Mom did see me in the city of St. Catherine, she crossed the street to avoid speaking to me. I had become an alcoholic—a drunk who slept in parked cars and lived in hobo jungles—a misfit."

Garry fell prey to poverty and the life of the streets. He was in and out of jail three times, and was finally put in prison on charges of petty theft.

"I had no standards—no moral standards—and was struggling to understand the world and what made it go around and how I fit into it," Garry said with tears in his eyes. "What was right—or wrong? I didn't know. I learned about life in hobo jungles, I learned from other broken people how to do things like make toast in prison by starting a fire in the toilet. Many of the men I met in prison and on the street became father figures to me. I was trying to learn about life from people who were messed up, and I had a lot of trouble come from that. When I got out of prison, I was 21 years old."

The Garry I knew did not fit at all with the young man whom Garry was painfully describing. He spoke of his first marriage to another broken person, who had also come from a fractured family and who had a violent alcoholic father who sexually abused her. This woman met Garry soon after his release from prison, and he was attracted to her strong survival skills. He desperately wanted to stay out of jail, and he thought she would provide him with willpower from out of her own moxie. Together, he hoped, they would find a new life. They started dating, and soon she became pregnant. Garry married his young pregnant girlfriend, but the baby she carried was born dead.

"I had an awful time with that. I woke up weeping for the baby for days…it's hard to think about that now…" He stopped for a moment. "I thought the right thing to do was to stick with her, right? We were both a couple of misfits who were hanging onto life by our fingernails, but then, when I was 26 years old, I got sober in AA, and things became very strained between us."

Garry began to put his life back together, going back to school and getting both his high-school diploma and a university degree. His job at General Motors took off, and Garry's hard work and natural charisma helped him be promoted. He worked as a foreman and from there on up the ladder. However, his intense time studying and working kept him away from home, away from his young children and very messed-up wife.

"I had this burden that I just didn't fit in and I wanted so much to be accepted. I had to have money," Garry told me. "Money was the thing that would make me acceptable to people around me, and that is what drove my decisions. If I could keep getting better jobs, get enough money, get things everyone else had…My wife and I started accumulating stuff! We had a house, two cars in the driveway, five children, and my job. I was sober and trying to go in one direction while she was drinking and going in the opposite direction."

Much to Garry's dismay, he discovered that his wife was whipping, beating, and physically abusing her sons (she had a special hatred for men because of her abusive father). She tried to get Garry to begin drinking again. Finally, Garry had had enough. They got a divorce, which was followed by an annulment from the Catholic Church.

"The divorce really set me off on another course of trying to put my life together again," Garry said. "I got really sick, got ulcers, lost a lot of weight. I knew how to work at GM, but emotionally I was a cripple. I would see my children—I went to rescue them at one point, and I bought a house for them to live with me."

After a series of ugly events with the police involved—and the kids getting into trouble with the law—the agency in charge determined that Garry would have custody of the children. "It was tough," Garry said. "They came to live with me as they were trying to figure out what was going on in their lives. They were emotional, and they were hurt. I don't know what kind of father I was—probably not that great because I was still trying to figure out what was going on myself."

GARRY WAS AWARE OF A "HIGHER POWER" through his AA meetings, but in a search for more he consulted soothsayers and fortune-tellers and got involved in the New Age movement. At one point, he would drive five hours back and forth to visit a fortune-teller in Ottawa, looking for some spiritual foundation. Physically he was getting weaker, and since he was finding no relief spiritually, he relented when his ex-wife came back into the picture. She said she was sober, had no men in her life, and wanted to have her children back for the summer.

"I went to the boys and asked if they would go and spend the time with their mother. Of course they were afraid of her," Garry said. "I talked them into it and told them they would be back with me in the fall."

But Garry's children never came back to him. His ex-wife went to court and regained full custody. Garry said it still hurts when he wonders whether the children ever fully understood the legal hassles he went through to get them back, and if they know how much he loves them.

With his children gone, Garry fell into an emotional black hole. He fell on his knees and cried out, "God, I can't do this anymore. I can't face another day. I can't go to GM one more day, God—I'm finished, I'm washed up, I'm a misfit, I've never done anything right…I just want to die!"

Because he was raised as a Catholic, Garry admits that he was afraid to commit suicide, but his will to live was going—was nearly gone. It was then he felt God began to answer his prayers. A friend who'd previously worked at GM with Garry suddenly turned up. This man had quit work after he had been through a divorce and had fled the country to avoid paying child support and alimony. Unexpectedly he called Garry saying, "I want to talk to you! I have something to share with you and I'm not really sure why, but I feel like we should have lunch."

Garry met his friend at a restaurant on the Canadian side of Niagara Falls. His friend was nearly manic with excitement, and he began to tell Garry about Jesus Christ. "He's telling me his testimony, and I'm listening to him and thinking, *Oh, great, this is all I need,*" Garry said. *"Now I've got a Jesus freak on my hands. I'm falling apart at the seams and now I've got this lunatic here."*

Garry told his friend he'd heard it all in jail. "George Beverly Shea had actually come to the prison once, and while he was singing, I almost went forward, but I couldn't get up the will to do it because of all the peer pressure in that prison atmosphere," Garry said. (Interestingly, Garry later met Shea through his work, and they eventually became close friends.) Garry told his friend thanks, but no thanks. "I said I was glad it had worked for him, but it wouldn't work for me." But his friend didn't let up. He gave Garry a popular book by Hal Lindsey called *The Late Great Planet Earth.*

LINDSEY'S BOOK STIRRED SOMETHING in Garry's heart. The prophecies in the book seemed to line up with and validate what Garry had read in the Bible. Garry decided to give his crazy, Jesus-freak friend a try. At a Catholic retreat house in Mt. Carmel, he took a recovery course about new beginnings for separated, widowed, and divorced people who had suffered great loss.

"What I learned was earth-shattering for me, and I began to understand some spiritual principles and how to heal some of my wounds by turning things over to Christ. I began to feel the grace of God," Garry said. "These people at the retreat house were so compassionate and understanding. I began to think about becoming a monk!" He laughed and continued. "There was such a peace about the place and, you know me, I don't do anything halfway. So I did wind up as a team member for the retreat, going back two or three times a year to help conduct the seminars."

However, Garry's wounds were deep, and there were many places in his life that were still untouched by the power of Jesus. There were amends to be made, and with every few steps forward, he slid a few steps back.

A new Christian, Garry studied his Bible daily, with a vengeance. Before allowing the grace of God to flood his soul, he took up the burden of perfection and works, which nearly killed him.

"I came home one night after being at a Christian meeting knowing I couldn't be a perfect person. I threw the Bible in the trash can and said to God, 'I can't be this person! I've failed at this! I can't be your man! I'm not put together that way!' And I fell on the bed and cried and cried, and that's the time I had this impression of God saying to me, 'I'm crying with you.' He felt my pain and brokenness."

Over the years Garry moved closer to this Jesus who knew his grief and suffering, and he found himself getting stronger and becoming more at peace. He met and married Veronica, and with her encouragement, he began to reach out to a family he longed to see.

Garry's older brother had left home at age 15, and his younger brother had left soon after. Knowing he had caused great embarrassment to his family, Garry was determined to apologize and ask for forgiveness.

Garry's older brother, Jim, had married well and had become a successful executive. Garry went to his home and knocked on the door. When Jim opened it, Garry said, "Jim, I know I've caused you a lot of embarrassment and problems because of my behavior. I want to apologize."

Garry said that Jim looked him full in the face and responded, "All your life you thought you got away with a lot of things. You never got away with anything. It's in your face and it's in your eyes." He shut the door in Garry's face.

Garry paused, sighed, and then told me, "On Jim's death-bed—he had cancer—I asked him if I could pray with him. I know that in heaven we'll have a lot of time. Someday we'll be brothers there. That was one opportunity to make things right...and there will be others to come."

Man is born broken. He lives by mending. The grace of God is the glue.

EUGENE O'NEILL

Chapter Fifteen

HOME WASN'T HOME WITHOUT HIM

The Prodigal Son's Father

I REMEMBER LEAVING NASHVILLE FOR NEW YORK *when I was 19 years old. Lacking a great inheritance, I was determined to make my own by singing in nightclubs. After I had made enough money, my plan was to study acting in this mecca of Broadway musicals and stake my claim in the world of theater. Did I ask God for His thoughts about my agenda? No, off I went…into a faraway land.*

And within a year-and-a-half, I returned home to my family—tired and worn-out, with little to show for my journeys except the knowledge that singing in smoky clubs was no way for my heart and spirit to grow. (It was the mercy of God—and many angels—that protected me from my own naïveté. Thankfully, I maintained my faith through these harrowing travels.) My earthly family welcomed me back with open arms and great relief, and God honored my return by bringing into my life many opportunities to keep on acting and singing, and eventually I found a career in Christian music.

So much love this prodigal daughter's parents had…So much like the loving father of the prodigal son…

The story of the prodigal son (Luke 15) has been written about and sung about, has inspired paintings and sermons, has been dissected over and over again through the centuries. There is much speculation about the wayward son's agony...his poor choices...his remorse and return home. Yet I wonder at what the father was thinking as he sent his son off into the unknown world that waited to take him on.

What can we learn of God's heart in this amazing story in Luke? Read on...

WHEN MY YOUNGER SON ASKED FOR his inheritance, I could see the proud, arrogant glint of youth in his eyes.

My older son, being more responsible perhaps, was much more the type to save his share of the property until he felt safe enough to invest it wisely. Perhaps his caution came with being the older—he seemed quite threatened, quite put off by his younger brother's ambition to take on the world.

"It's time for me to grow up now, Father, and get on with my life. There is so much I haven't seen and done, and I want to start enjoying life now. Please give me what is mine, and then I'll be on my way." His eyes flickered with the head-strong spirit he'd had from birth.

As my youngest started down that road, he assured me that I wouldn't see him for a long time. He was headed for far-off places that promised the adventures he longed to experience. All I could do was let him go. He never saw the tears I held back, or heard the prayers I prayed every day and night on his behalf.

I love both of my sons equally, although each is cut from a different cloth, and I've never demanded allegiance to our family from either of them. I wasn't about to start now, with my younger son's departure. His life would be his to carve out. But he took a part of my heart with him. My love would be a hidden treasure in his knapsack, always within his grasp when he needed it.

We heard stories of my younger one's reckless forays into "experiencing the world." He was roaming from bed to bed, town to town, bar to marketplace, spending his money until, at last, he had none. Even poverty didn't put a damper on his quest. He was charming, and he lived off others for a while. But at last even his charisma fell flat.

With all the pieces of news that came to me, firsthand, secondhand, who knew what to believe? I ached to see him. Often I would turn my face away so that no one could see the grief in my soul. Oh that my precious son would just come home! That was all I prayed for, all I wanted. To see his face again and to hold him in my arms.

When we heard that he'd taken a job feeding pigs, I knew that his pain must be far worse than mine. My handsome, strong, proud son would have laughed if anyone had suggested, years earlier, that he might be so employed. Then came one of the ugliest rumors—he was so hungry that he had asked to eat the pods that the pigs were fed, but had been refused.

Ironically, at this most brutal news I began to have hope that my son might return home! How much worse could things be? It's odd to admit, but from that day forward, I began to look for him at the outskirts of our property, every day. Somehow I could feel him returning. For what seemed like weeks, I was ready to meet him at any moment, eager to rush out at the first sign of his appearance.

Finally there came the day I had so longed for. My son's figure was just a dot on the horizon, but I knew it was him. I could tell by the way he moved. I knew everything about him—and this was my dear son coming back to us.

My elder son thought I had lost my mind. The servants smiled with compassion at my insistence that they start preparing a meal. I could not take my eyes off the figure approaching our home.

While he was still far away, I rushed out the front door and ran down the road to meet him. My legs were filled with strength, and my body was on fire with excitement. I couldn't contain my joy! My tears fell, and at last my son limped toward me, his head hung low. "Father, I have sinned against you and against God!" he cried, falling to grasp my knees. "I've lost everything! I am not worthy for you to receive me! I am nothing…nothing…"

His words went on through the weeping, and I'm not sure he knew what was happening as I kissed his head, drew him close, and helped him back to our house. Commanding the servants to prepare a great celebration, I put my hand on my son's dusty shoulder and finally calmed his sobbing.

"My son was dead, and now he is alive again!" I picked him up almost like when he was a little boy and swung him around in a circle. Laughing out loud, I said, "He was lost, but now he is found! Bring out the best clothes of mine—hurry, give him something fine to wear!"

Food and wine and music and the companionship of my family have never been sweeter than on that day when my beloved son returned home to us. Yes, my elder son and I faced some difficulty between us because there was no punishment for his younger brother's disloyalty. I understand how that must have angered him. He refused to eat the first meal with us. And I have tried to help him accept the fact that I love and adore him no less than his younger brother. But my elder son never left me—he was never lost and filled with remorse. All I had was his, and he freely shared it with me.

We had much to celebrate in receiving his younger brother back. For there was a time, I feared, he might not choose to return.

It took my younger son quite by surprise that he was so gloriously met. His past foolishness could not compare to the beauty of him—his personhood—and all that he had learned. It didn't matter—the lost money, the lost years, they all found their way full circle back to us because we were together again at last.

And home just wasn't home without him.

Can I Love Other Messy People?

The landscape of the American church is littered
with burned-out bodies and abortive ministries born
of unhealthy guilt and fear of resisting God's will.

BRENNAN MANNING,
from *Reflections for Ragamuffins*

Chapter Sixteen

THE PHARISEE IN ME

Bonnie's Story

WELL, WELL, WELL.

I was taught, long ago, that most of you who might be reading this book are going to hell, hell, hell.

I'm referring here to the Christian readers—not the ones who have yet to decide for themselves whether to choose or reject the message of the gospel, but the Christ-believers who don't approach Him in the "correct way."

I can hardly believe I'm writing this.

But it's the ugly truth.

My childhood church experiences nearly ruined my life. I don't blame the well-intentioned, God-fearing, loving people who filled the pews. I do, however, continue to recover from the years of theology that filled me with a hefty fear of God but left me with little knowledge about His radical grace. The assortment of teaching I heard ran the gamut from being a terrific substitute for anesthesia to being an effective replacement for torture with bamboo shoots under the fingernails. Hopelessly helpless in this kind of atmosphere, I began having migraine headaches at age six, and they continued into my early 20s. I soaked in all the guilt, all the "unworthiness" from what I heard and never felt like I would measure up to being someone God could love.

Compounding this anxiety was my passion for the arts. There was no room in my church to use my talents—no choir, musical instruments, or soloists. Sadly, there was a stifling atmosphere of condemnation that left little room for my dreams of using my gifts for Christ.

Thank God above that I was delivered from such deadly theology in my late teens. I was well into college before I understood that God came to Earth to wear human skin through the life of His Son, and would go to any lengths to help me through this messy world. Despite this, I know the Pharisee in me lies dormant, ever ready to spring awake if I allow it.

⸺

Some time ago I received a heart-wrenching e-mail from a woman named Stacy. Stacy is desperately searching for a way to comprehend that God truly loves her. Is she a drug addict? Has she been a wild woman—promiscuous, alcoholic? Has her life been just one miserable failure after another? Is she a prodigal daughter, filled with shame that she's brought down on herself? Have her choices to turn a stubborn back on God led her to feel unloved?

No, Stacy was simply raised in a church that taught all about law and little about love. Seeds of unworthiness were planted in her heart when she was a child and now have sprouted and grown into a strangling vine. Stacy feels like she cannot be or do what God requires of her. Her letters to me tell of a tug-of-war that rages in her between wanting to know God personally and being ashamed of questioning the icy absolutes that were heaped upon her from birth as to how she must serve Jesus. "Don't question anything." "Don't rock the boat." "Don't challenge what you've been taught, for God will surely be displeased with such behavior, and you don't want to push Him over the edge." These messages leave no room for her humanness, for the untidy areas of her life. Where does Stacy take her disappointments, when she feels as if she is inadequate even to pray?

At an early age, Stacy's church stamped fear into her heart, but left out the mark of grace—the grace given to her through Christ's death. She is an adult now, searching the Word of God, dog-paddling like mad in a sea of legalistic theology that is always trying to pull her under to drown in defeat. When she writes to me, she asks for prayer. Although she's been told that crying is wrong, she wants to one day feel loved enough to weep before her Father. I told her that God is so crazy about her that He wants her to feel free enough to crawl up into His lap and cry big, sloppy mascara marks down His robe!

HER WORDS RESONATE IN MY OWN HEART. Her pain leaves me livid at the baggage-laden, well-meaning, utterly misguided preachers and teachers who take innocent children and give them a works-based, fear-filled "religion." My ugly, graceless reactions to this come both from my own background and also from the years I have railed against the poisonous legalistic theology that I was handed.

Raised in a strict, legalistic church, I was taught as a small child that there was only one way to heaven—the way *our* church made the journey. All other religions were wrong, even if their members professed to love Jesus as their Savior. It was our way or the highway—to hell. Any change in biblical interpretation or arrangement of service, any new ideas, any instrumental music, even any change in mode of dress, was prohibited. The grown-ups around me spoke of other people who had problems in their lives as if they had died. "Well...I'm just shocked! Well, of course they won't be back!" And on the occasion of a funeral I might hear, "I hope they *really* knew Jesus...baptized in time and all that, you know. I'm not sure if they will make it..."

At my childhood church, you could never really be sure of anything except that *we* were the ones on the inside track to God. We could judge whether or not someone else was going to "make it." And yet, even on the inside track, we could never be certain that God loved us enough for us to "make it." You just lived by the skin of your teeth. There was little grace; rather, there was static faith, rules, and a rigid "punching of the time clock" three times a week—be in that pew or else. Fear upon fear upon fear.

I became a Christian at the age of 12, mostly out of apprehension that if I didn't become one I would go up in flames before I hit 13. Jesus taught in the temple at age 12, so I was told that my sins began to pile up—on the record—at that magical milestone. The loving heavenly Father who gave His Son, who gave mercy to all mankind, was not on the agenda. I had to be perfect as God was perfect. How this would realistically happen was never explained. "Just do it," I was told. (Nike would have loved my church!)

My current pastor, Scotty Smith, pointed out something very different. In the story of the father who welcomed home his boy—the parable of the prodigal son—God laces up His Nikes long before we do and races out to greet us while we are still far away (Luke 15). The grace of God moves to seek us, to gather us to the heart of God in Christ, *because* He knows we cannot "just do it!" Unfortunately, all I recall being told was to pull myself up by my own bootstraps and pray to an angry God who might or might not accept me. It all depended on my performance. What a terrifying proposition.

I began to view the world in the way I was taught. Shape up, look good on the outside, cover up anything unmentionable, don't ask questions, and pray, pray, pray—that God would somehow find a way to stomach me. I began to stink of self-righteousness.

During my teen years, I felt a great deal of turmoil in my heart. Many of my best friends were other Christians who did not attend my particular denomination. Privately I would pray that God would spare them from a fiery eternity because I knew they meant well. And silently I carried a burden for them—almost like knowing beforehand the timing and details of their deaths, yet unable to prevent them.

I had this tremendous desire to take my friends into a room and say, "You guys are going to go to hell because your church isn't the 'right' denomination! I know the end of your story. Now quick, while there's time, make a change!" Perhaps I did actually preach a bit of this to them from time to time, but thankfully no one took me seriously.

~

IT WASN'T UNTIL I WAS IN MY LATE TEENS that I began to study the Word of God more closely, without the constant bell of "condemnation theology" ringing in my ears. It's impossible to describe the astonishment and gratitude I experienced as grace began to wrap itself around my life. As I opened my heart to the Lord's acts of great love and His words of mercy, I discovered a Jesus that I had never known.

This Jesus was a passionate lover of all men and women. This Jesus loved the ones the world called "losers," the one who fell glaringly short of any notion of perfection.

This Jesus was a man—and yet He was the heart of God.

This Jesus reached out to everyone He could find—to His people, the Jews—to the lost and the desolate, to robbers, to His enemies. He even opened His inner circle to a man destined to betray Him to His death.

In short, Jesus loved sinners! They needed no other credentials!

The Bible didn't specify a holy path to the cross, it simply reminded me over and over again how my life was changed forever because Christ had chosen to pay for all I could not and would not ever be. There was no shame, just statements about the obvious need of us all to be reconciled to God. I read in 2 Corinthians 5:21, "For our sake he made him to be sin who knew no sin, so that in him we might become the righteousness of God." Jesus said, "If I am lifted up I will draw all men to me." He proclaimed that He was the way, the truth, and the life. Any that believed in Him as the Son of God would live in no condemnation.

What a soul-full of relief flooded through me!

I took off the judge's robes. Hung them up forever in the Pharisee closet and vowed I'd never wear those heavy garments of death again. Yet surprisingly, that hideous closet door threatens to creak open from time to time, and those straitjacket robes are still hanging there, as starched and constricting as ever. Taught from birth that everyone else was wrong, that failures in one's life would require a death sentence, that most likely even I would never make it to heaven unless I earned my way somehow, I carry a deep imprint of Pharisee-ness in my mind.

For now, I continually slam the door shut, lock it, try to throw the key away. Like in a horror film, that key still shows up on occasion, no matter what lengths I go to destroy it. But Jesus now holds the keys to death, and I know He has the key to this door in His hands as well.

Now I battle anger because of those years of denominational imprisonment. It's like pushing a button: When I hear rhetoric that condemns others because of the way they approach a worship service or because they allow musicians to sing or play instruments, I get mad. When I hear people decide that some peripheral issue that has nothing to do with the cross should merit a 12-week study by the Sunday-school class, I get mad.

I have to constantly pray to forgive the people who put this religious monkey on my back when I was a child. After migraines, divorce, single parenthood, depression, and now a second marriage, I've been allowed a personal discovery of the true heart of freedom in Christ. Years of suffering have opened the gates of forgiveness and grace for me. But still, I have a facial-tic, stomach-lurching response to legalism wherever it rears its ugly head.

*

WHEN I OBSERVE HOW JESUS RESPONDED to the Pharisees, Sadducees, and other groups of men who controlled the Jews with their decrees, I see a passionate Christ who showed, in rare instances, a very human anger.

Christ was profoundly patient with the messiest people around: prostitutes, Gentiles, Roman guards. Even the thief on the cross next to Jesus, as he hung between heaven and Earth dying, heard words of comfort, forgiveness, and hope.

Jesus had come to this Earth to live as one of us, to free us from the bondage of laws that cannot be kept. It took His own blood to build the bridge back to the Father. He was outraged at the hypocrisy of the Jewish leaders of the day. Evidently, they were a lot like some of our leaders now who have become intoxicated with power and wealth.

When Jesus entered the temple in Jerusalem and proceeded to turn over the tables in an outburst of pain and indignation, it was not because the buying and selling were desecrating His Father's house. Rather it was because of this: The Jewish law required people to have certain doves and lambs to offer before the Lord. The merchants had set up shop in front of the temple and were charging far more money than was right for what they knew the people had to have. Those who were there to worship God were being taken advantage of by men who were out for a quick extra buck.

The laws of God had been turned into a means of profiteering—by men who would stand on corners and pray great prayers, then silently rob the poor, the widows, and less fortunate. Nothing tore at the heart of God in Jesus more than watching men misrepresent Him with lies, oppression of others, thievery, and deceit.

Jesus called these men hypocrites, vipers, and false prophets. They had the truth of God given to them in Scripture. They had the power to show others the way. But they controlled the masses and protected their own health and wealth by using fear.

RECENTLY I SANG AT A DEAR FRIEND'S WEDDING. She was married in a denominational church similar to the one of my childhood. When I arrived, I breathed a huge sigh of relief when I saw that a keyboard was at the rehearsal and that I wouldn't be singing a capella for the entire service. The keyboardist and I had a great time together, and she shared with me her bewilderment over why this church allowed a piano in the sanctuary for weddings but not for church services. She offered the following explanation, which was given to her by a law-bound groom when she posed the question at another such wedding: "He said that it's all right to have instruments used in weddings because the wedding service is not considered sacred."

My mouth hung open. I thought I'd heard it all.

I cannot tell you how hard I clenched my fist to keep from screaming. Feeling the blood rush to my face, thankfully I opted to laugh. There just isn't an intelligent way to justify manmade absolutes. With all its promises for security, the closer in you move to inspect legalism, the more obvious are the inconsistencies, the cracks in the plaster, the leaky faucet that still drips, drips, drips…"You can never measure up"… "Remove this instrument, remove this person, this tradition, this type of building, this hymn"…"Do not change anything! We are right, we *must* be right! If anything changes, the house of cards falls, and that *must* not happen."

When will it be clear that the miracle, the mystery, the saving power of Jesus is not to be found in the law? He came to complete and fulfill the law. And He died to set man free from such law. Holding innocent hearts to a rigid, law-polluted theology makes a mockery of all that Christ suffered through on the cross. How Jesus must shake His head and weep for those who profess to have faith, yet chain themselves to laws they cannot keep—living in fear and dread when He offers security and forgiveness.

I've been all over the world, singing in churches of every type of denomination imaginable. No one church does things the exact same way as another. In one instance, after we had led praise songs in the Sunday morning service, communion was offered. I stood to get in line, when Marty McCall, my partner in First Call, quietly pulled me back into my seat.

"What's the deal?" I asked.

He whispered, "You can't take communion here."

"Why not?" I replied. After all, we had just led the church in worship.

"You aren't a member of this denomination," Marty said. He pointed to the fine print on the bottom of the church bulletin, which stated that unless one were a _____ by denomination, then "please do not participate in the communion service."

Somehow, this church, full of wonderful people, could justify paying First Call to come and lead their people in praising God in song but, because we were not affiliated with their denomination, not allow us to take communion. All of us call Christ our Savior, yet that still isn't enough.

I try to keep my sense of humor.

Perhaps there is much to be learned from the words of Albert Camus, who wrote, "The only way to deal with an unfree world is to become so absolutely free that your very act of existence becomes an act of rebellion." Follow this with the words of Paul from 1 Corinthians 9:19: "Though I am free and belong to no man, I make myself a slave to everyone, to win as many as possible" (NIV).

Freedom was paid for at the cross of Christ, an unearned gift to be guarded, respected, and enjoyed. Legalism leads to fear. We all make mistakes, and the chains of legalism remind us over and over how we fail to live up to the mark. Legalism is the thumb pinning down, mashing, the spirit and the soul.

I see so many people afraid to live for fear they might actually enjoy life! Yet Jesus said that He came to earth to bring us life in all its abundance.

May we all dance, sing, praise Him, and love Him with our whole being.

And when we hurt, may we know that we can run down the hall to our Father's room, tap Him on the shoulder, crawl up in His lap, and cry our human tears on His royal robes.

*P*erhaps any homosexual who humbly accepts his cross and puts himself under Divine guidance will be shown the way. Like all other tribulations, it must be offered to God and His guidance—how to use it must be sought.

C.S. Lewis,
as quoted in *A Severe Mercy* by Sheldon Vanauken

Chapter Seventeen

REAL TEARS

Tim's Story

I HAVE MANY HOMOSEXUAL FRIENDS. I do not approve of or even understand their choices, in the same way that I feel disheartened when anyone, myself included, chooses to live in a manner that grieves the spirit of God and tramples on the tremendous grace of Jesus. But I cannot deny my affection for these friends who have the burden of homosexual yearnings, and my love for who they are at the core of their unguarded selves.

We have been honest with one another for more than two decades, vehemently arguing our own viewpoint of where God would wish to see us all sexually whole before Him. Through it all, our loyalties to each other as fellow human beings and true friends have survived our agreements to disagree. These friends know where I stand and what I believe the Lord God desires for them, but they also know that my love and prayers for them are rock-solid.

Some of these dear ones in my life who deal with homosexuality have chosen a conventional, heterosexual marriage, have chosen to have children and daily ask God for grace. Others are questioning and aren't sure what to do. Finally there are friends of mine who stand firmly in the belief that they are Christians who walk the road of an openly gay lifestyle. Obviously, it's easy for judgmental thoughts to jump into my head; it's easy for me to start ranting and raving about how I should "give up on" the ones who are shamelessly gay and pray only for the ones who are attempting to change.

However, knowing full well the capacity I have—and my heterosexual friends have—to fall short of what God asks, I find little reason to differentiate between gay and straight in my prayers for fidelity to what would please God. How do we bring honor to Jesus with our sexual choices? Infidelity to Jesus with one's body is the same, whether one feels like a heterosexual or a homosexual, whether one is married or single, whether one considers oneself gay or straight. All fall short...all of us need to keep our eyes and thoughts on Jesus and His lordship.

In the book *This Is My Destiny*, songwriter-author Dennis Jernigan openly writes of his deliverance from a homosexual lifestyle:

> *My identity began early in life. A boy who could play the piano, a deep emotional awareness of what was going on around me, a distant relationship with my earthly father...the Enemy of God capitalized upon this belief...*
>
> *All sin is the same. It separates us from God. And in every case, the remedy is the same. We all need a Savior; we need Jesus Christ.*

Shame and defeat mark the inner lives of many who battle homosexuality in their search for God's peace. Further condemnation, it seems to me, would drive them further into pain and despair. I have seen four homosexual friends of mine die needless deaths. Two were from suicide, two from their taking the wrong person home from the wrong place on the wrong night.

Real tears...I believe the ones who struggle honestly before God with their sexuality are people who cry real tears, for more reasons than I can imagine. How do they deal with these deep-seated longings that are death, that are taboo, no matter how the world chatters on about "political correctness" in lifestyles. How has the church dealt with this torment? How can I show God's love and compassion, yet not compromise on what I see as God's law?

When I ponder the question "What Would Jesus Do?" I believe He would speak truth to all men and women about sexuality and look for any way to restore their loss of self-esteem with His love and humanity. Did He not reach out to the adulterer, the woman living with a man out of wedlock, the blind, the deaf, the paralyzed, the hopeless ones all around Him?

Christ did not die for one group of people, for one list of offenses—certain specialized sins—and then somehow miraculously withhold other drops of His blood away from others, those branded as beyond grace. The cross of Christ stands to offer new life, new hope, new grace wherever its shadow falls.

MY DEAR FRIEND TIM HAS THE COURAGE to be achingly honest about his past, his present, and his future hope in Christ. He admits to being drawn to men physically. His story tells why.

Tim grew up in a large city in Texas, where his father was a preacher for a very conservative, fundamental Southern denomination. To the community, Tim was part of an all-American "perfect family." But it was a façade. Tim told me, "The beatings were regular and not regulated in duration or severity. There was always a reason…talking in church, bad grades, having an opinion."

Tim told me that one Sunday morning he was dressed and ready for church. His father began beating him. "I began yelling at Dad that if he didn't stop hitting me I would tell everyone at church that he smoked," Tim said. "My brother had recently shown me the 'secret' place that held cigarettes and alcohol. Dad stopped for a second, and I looked up into his face. His belt was raised over his head, and I detected a moment of regret. Then he proceeded to administer the punishment with added fury."

When Tim's father finally stopped beating him, Tim walked into the bathroom to wash his face and to check in the mirror for any visible marks that would be seen by his friends at church. His mother told him she was ashamed of him and that he should go and apologize to his dad.

"Hardly a day went by when I wasn't reminded by my father that I was stupid and worthless, and that I took after my mom's side of the family and would always be ugly," Tim told me. "There were times when I knew that a beating was coming and would determine that I *would not* cry. However, if I fought back the tears, Mother would stop spanking me and slap me across the face until she was satisfied that the tears were flowing freely enough."

As a child at the mercy of whatever his family allotted to him, Tim thought that the cruelty of his home life was normal. At the tender age of eight, Tim felt the mercy of Jesus tugging at his heart. Full of excitement, he asked his father to perform the baptism ceremony. His father refused. He told Tim he was too young and needed to wait. Until he was 11, Tim sat in church longing to be baptized, hearing sermons about how he was doomed to hell unless he was baptized, filled with fear that he might not be immersed in time. Finally, Tim convinced his father to baptize him.

"After the baptism, I felt so full that I couldn't stop the tears from flowing. My godfather hugged me, but then my dad walked by and sneered and asked, 'What are you crying for?' Fortunately for me, my godfather had a sense of the moment and replied, 'This is important. If he wants to cry, he can cry.'"

Tim's father's church grew by leaps and bounds, and his dad was away from home more and more attending to necessary church work. But the beatings continued, worked in between supper and meetings. Trips to church on Sunday mornings grew more volatile, often filled with explosive interaction between his parents. His mother accused his father of infidelities. Finally, his parents divorced.

TIM'S BATTLE WITH HOMOSEXUAL FEELINGS began in junior high and high school when he realized he had always been attracted to men. In an effort to be accepted, he discovered a talent for making people laugh. Everyone liked him because he was a "walking party." Tim hid his self-loathing and fear behind a façade of laughter. "No matter how much fun I was having, I always had to go home," Tim said. "I never allowed myself to explore my feelings for men. I kept all emotion locked away."

In the rigid religious denomination Tim grew up in, there was not much room for grace, perhaps not any. Tim worked as hard as he could to earn his way into heaven. "I pleaded with and tried to negotiate with God about my sexu-ality," Tim said. "But the desires would not go away." Although Tim had determined that he would spend eternity in hell, he still decided he would spend his life loving God. "My prayer stopped being, 'How much do I need to do to be saved?' and turned into 'Isn't there anything I can do to be saved?'" He didn't believe God could love him as a homosexual.

But Tim's willingness to serve a God who he believed would never accept him kept him on a path to finding the mercy of Jesus. And Jesus was there all along, yearning for Tim to find the truth of His endless love.

Tim's struggles went on through his parents' divorce and into college. One semester shy of graduation, he dropped out of college. He went to Nashville, where his life soon revolved around acting, theater, study, singing, and church work. Slowly, the grace of God became a part of his vocabulary.

Although Tim didn't act on his sexual preferences, he decided to "come out of the closet." But he lived in fear of his own desires and was afraid to have male friends. "In fact, certain men who found out that I was gay turned their back on me...a common occurrence," Tim recalled. He began to disconnect from people. "If someone forced me to go to a party or any place where there were more than two or three people, I would get nauseated and break out into a cold sweat. Then I'd retreat to a corner and do everything I could think of to leave early."

He moved to California to pursue acting, and there he discovered the Internet. Soon he was meeting men in chat rooms who he felt understood him. He'd then invite them over for the night. "At first there was excruciating guilt and the determination never to go there again," Tim recalled. But over time, it got easier. "For a few hours I was important to someone. For a few hours I wasn't ugly. And during those hours, it was worth the risk." Tim was soon addicted to the counterfeit acceptance of the gay community he could access online. When he moved to Arkansas, he found a new "market" of men. Yet, even in the midst of his rebellion, Tim's heart ached for God's help.

"I kept asking God to forgive me and prayed that His grace would be big enough to cover my stupidity and arrogance and selfishness. I realized I was constantly slapping Him in the face, but on another level I was thinking that He should have never made me this way and it was His fault. I continued in the belief that I was unlovable and not worth spending time on.

"But God continued to love me, and He began to place people, even men, into my life who would love me as well. My best friend is one of those men." Tim said he told this man "flat out" that they would never be friends. They were too different. "He was a California-type surfer dude, a self-proclaimed 'chick-magnet,'" Tim remembers. "I was a decade older, ugly, stupid, gay—and we had absolutely nothing in common except our church."

Even when Tim told the man to leave him alone, he refused. "He would call or just show up and take me to dinner or church or a movie," Tim said. "He would take the constant ridicule I heaped on him. I used everything in my arsenal to sabotage the friendship. But he never left."

⸎

AND THEN TIM'S PRAYERS WERE ANSWERED.

"The icy winter that had gripped my heart for so many years was slowly beginning to thaw. I was horrified of my feelings and would retreat time and time again. But my friend would not give up."

Tim's best friend eventually married and moved to Denver. They still keep in touch, and "my friend never ends a conversation without telling me that he loves me," Tim said. "Even when I am having a bad day, he still refuses to give up."

The struggles with chat rooms continued for a while. But Tim found that the men he met through the Internet failed to fill the gaping hole in his life. Finally, the truth was seared into his heart: "As much as I loved Jesus and desired relationship with Him, I hadn't given myself totally to that relationship," Tim told me. "I hadn't sacrificed everything, and He knew it. In His ruthless determination to have me *totally* as His own, I recognized He had turned me over to a depraved mind."

At this point, Tim quotes a Scripture that almost every gay man I know—in rebellion against the Lord's words—has cast aside with some sort of dismissal. To my friend Tim, these words provided a portrait, an illumination, that allowed him to step back and see himself and his need for Jesus. That portrait reads,

> *Although they knew God, they neither glorified him as God nor gave thanks to him, but their thinking became futile and their foolish hearts were darkened…There-fore God gave them over in the sinful desires of their hearts to sexual impurity for the degrading of their bodies with one another. They exchanged the truth of God for a lie…Because of this, God gave them over to shameful lusts…Furthermore, since they did not think it worthwhile to retain the knowledge of God, he gave them over to a depraved mind, to do what ought not be done (Romans 1:21,24-25,26,28 NIV).*

The complete passage contains a blunt reference regarding homosexuality, but you could argue that God's giving us over to our shameful lusts and desires might encompass both heterosexual and homosexual choices. As a church, as a people seeking Jesus as our brother and Savior and One who loves us beyond loving, this chapter challenges each of us in our sexuality and in the integrity with which we choose to treat our bodies.

Clee

TIM'S OUTBURSTS OF EXCITEMENT ARE ALWAYS childlike in their intensity and purity. Whenever I hear from him about a new insight, a new vision, or a special time in his life, he never tells me about it without exclamation points! He describes the moment when God's love came to life for him: "I realized that God's absence from my heart meant that His love for me is so wild and extreme that He would be bold enough to turn me over to my sinful nature," Tim told me. "And being the truest lover of all, He reluctantly but resolutely stepped back and gave me the freedom to get burned! That truth broke my heart!"

Tim was at a spiritual high point, but he knew he couldn't stay there long without wanting to jump off the cliff. He called the counseling center of a large church and asked the receptionist if she knew of any support groups for gay Christians. She sort of stumbled around and said, "Um...well... hold on." She put the receiver down, and Tim heard her call, "Len...there's an oxymoron on the phone!" When Len picked up the receiver, he told Tim about a group called "Celebrate Recovery." Tim remembers the first night he went: "I was absolutely certain everyone in the room could hear my heart pounding. I was scared to death, wanted more than anything in life to turn and hightail it out of there—I felt God would surely receive me into heaven, since right then, I was in hell."

This group—without condemnation, and with love, grace, and forgiveness—became the body of Christ for Tim. They walked side by side with him in his healing, "affirming me as a man," he says, "not a label.

"They accepted my weakness because they are acutely aware of their own," Tim told me. "We have laughed together, cried together, yelled at each other, lifted each other up, pressed our thumbs down on each other when necessary, held each other to strict accountability…We have ached for each other, rejoiced with victories, and shown compassion when someone has exposed their own failures. We have taken judgment out of our vocabulary and have left it to God. We have accepted as we have been accepted. In short, we have experienced church—in what I believe is the truest and most distilled sense of the word."

~

JESUS—GOD IN THE FLESH—SHOWED the evidence of God's great love by reaching out to the "losers" in His culture. The Bible doesn't say whether or not He dealt with homosexuals, but it does show us how Christ openly loved women with terrible reputations and simple men who turned their backs on Him in His last hours on earth. With each of His words and actions, He sought them out, encouraged them to change their lives, forget the past, and find new grace in His love. I believe Jesus wants to have us be the evidence of His love to those who are trying, the ones who desire to change, the ones who have failed and are tormented by their mistakes.

Tim told me, "I have found how true a companion and comrade I have in Jesus. I find myself leaning toward His fantastic desire to be my buddy, my confidant, my pal. He is crazy about me. I no longer have to live in fear of being 'found out.' Being given the freedom of revealing myself to other men and women has liberated me in a way that I have never known. I have found that I can give myself away in relationships in a way that is more holy and right than I believed possible. Those men whom I truly love, I find myself not attracted to sexually. And the most astonishing discovery in this journey is that I can allow myself to be loved."

As people of faith, we are called to tear down the walls of bigotry and the system of which sins "really count." We are called to embrace all men and women in the love of God and show them a new way to freedom in Christ. I pray that I can show this kind of mercy to the "uglies," the undesirables, the misunderstood, the frightened, the hungry for affection in our culture.

In Tim's eloquent words: "Take heart, those of you who may just be starting this incredible adventure. It's hard work. But hopefully you will find what I am learning.

"Am I cured? No. However, I now recognize the truth— the weaknesses that once threatened to destroy me are the very same weaknesses God now uses to make me strong.

"Have I been delivered? Yes!

"I have been delivered—from the chains of loneliness, the prison of isolation, and the dark, dreary dread of an uncertain future—into the arms of a ridiculously wild, fiercely passionate, and outrageously unrestrained love affair with Jesus Christ. And every day...*every* day—even on the bad days—if I listen, I hear Him say, 'I am so very proud of you.' I stand before you now a trophy of Jesus Christ."

Tim has the brave-hearted faith to believe in what he cannot see...that God loves him in this struggle and will see him through to the other side.

I was "handicapped" by fundamentalism, yes. But the handicap ultimately worked in such a way as to make me "poor in spirit," a state which Jesus described as a prerequisite for inheriting the kingdom of God.

PHILIP YANCEY,
from *I Was Just Wondering*

Chapter Eighteen

GUESS WHO'S COMING TO DINNER?

Zacchaeus

I'M ALMOST SIX FEET TALL. *I can sometimes see over entire rooms of people, depending on what shoes I'm wearing. In high school it was a curse. As an adult, I see it as a blessing.*

When I traveled to Asia with First Call, I passed by a booth of gawking women who according to our interpreter said, "She has much leg!"—as if I were a freak of nature. So, I find it difficult to relate to this man named Zacchaeus, who had to find a tree to climb in order to get a glimpse of Jesus when He came through town.

Zaccheus was a tax collector, one of the men most feared and hated by the Jews. He was rich and wealthy—he was everything that represented the oppression of the Romans. And he was short.

As a child in Sunday school, I sang a little song about him that I doubt he would appreciate:

> *Zacchaeus was a wee little man, and a wee little man was he...*

I always added "O!" and launched into "B–I–N–G–O, B–I–N–G–O, B–I–N–G–O, and BINGO was his NAME-O!"

(That's what growing up in the iron grip of legalism did to me. I lost a bit of my mind in the process.)

The Bible says in the book of Luke, chapter 19, that Zacchaeus was a small man, but one whose large heart was "desperate to see Jesus." Evidently he had no qualms about doing anything to accomplish his desire, so he found a sycamore tree located close to the action and climbed up as the parade passed by.

Jesus, never predictable, never one to miss the slightest movement of faith in action, noticed this small man in the tree and called out to him. "Zacchaeus, come down from there. I'm having dinner at your home tonight!"

Jesus had a tremendous sense of timing and humor. Imagine how Zacchaeus felt—his heart must have skipped a beat.

Jesus not only picked him, all alone sitting in a tree, out of an entire crowd of people, but He called Zacchaeus by name—and they had never met! Not only did Zacchaeus behold the Nazarene, but Jesus invited Himself into his home! This was bound to cause a huge uproar.

Zacchaeus was right on this count.

As usual, Jesus did the unexpected. He reached out to the one least likely to anticipate His touch. The people around Him threw a bloody fit.

But this man named Zacchaeus represents one of the ragtag group of people that Jesus came across and embraced because of their faith in who He was...because of their innocent courage to ask of Him the impossible, which He longed to give...so He could show over and over again without restraint how much of the world God loves: all of it.

Jesus the Christ, God on Earth, was a man who knew how it felt to climb a tree, to wish for more than what was visible, and to have a fire in His belly that changed the world.

So off to the home of Zacchaeus He went. (I find it hard to imagine that this visit was in His Day-Timer.) Read and see how God used this unpopular outcast...

I DIDN'T GIVE A SECOND THOUGHT to what any of these people were saying about me. I wanted to see the Nazarene. And there was such a commotion that day He arrived, so many people pushing and shoving and making a fuss. Being a man of small stature, but a reputable personage in my profession, I took it upon myself to find a tree suitable for climbing. I wanted to ensure myself a good look at this man who seemed to be standing the world on its head.

I heard the group traveling with the Nazarene long before I could see them. It was a hot day, and dust was filling the air as the crowd assembled. When the haze parted for a moment, I first caught sight of this holy man. Please forgive me for saying this so bluntly, but He really wasn't much to look at. He didn't wear the royal robes that one called Messiah—King of the Jews—ought to wear. And His band of followers were a sorry-looking bunch too.

However, as He moved closer to where I sat in a sycamore tree, I sensed something unusual about Him. The Nazarene had eyes that saw everything and everyone. He didn't just see us, He saw into who we were. His gaze wasn't one of self-righteousness—not the kind of look the Jewish leaders gave me. How well I knew what they thought of me—the disdain on their faces was as clear as the midnight stars.

No, this Jesus of Nazareth, He looked at everyone with eyes full of compelling care. He drew everyone to Him with one glance—blindingly, searingly loving. I couldn't take my eyes off Him.

Suddenly, much to my surprise, He looked up into the tree at me, and called me by name!

I almost fell headfirst, right there on the spot! We had never met, but He called to me as if I were someone He'd known all His life. In a few words that seemed to hang in the air forever, He announced, "Zacchaeus, hurry down from there. I'm coming to your home tonight to be your guest!"

For an instant I was too stunned to move. Then I scrambled down from my perch and led the Nazarene to my home.

Oh, if only you could have heard the comments that were building to a fevered pitch. "What business does He have getting cozy with this crook?" a shrill voice to my left called.

"Master—" I stumbled a bit over my words as I stood before Him, trying to somehow merit His attention—"I give away half of my income to the poor—and if I'm caught cheating, I will pay four times the damages."

I wanted Him to see into my heart, past my vocation. For I did feel a longing to assist those less fortunate than me, and I had done so quietly in the past.

The Nazarene smiled, looked at me like no one has ever looked before or since, and raised His arms above His head. "Today is salvation day in this home! Here he is: Zacchaeus, son of Abraham! For the Son of Man came to find and restore the lost."

He was smiling, laughing, hugging me and those around Him as we journeyed to my home. All I could do was think, *"Son of Abraham?"* I'd been called a lot of names in my life, but nothing close to this. He was acknowledging me as part of the blessed line of Abraham!

The Jewish people hated me—didn't He know this? I collected their dreadful taxes and cut deals with as many as I could, always trying to make things as easy as possible for the most unfortunate. But we tax collectors were the "enemies of the people," the "puppets of Rome." We were dog's meat in the eyes of our nation.

But this man's words ran through my soul and into my spirit like a sword of merciful light. If the Nazarene could call me His brother in Abraham, then I would gladly accept such an inheritance!

There's never been a night to compare with the company, companionship, and joy of that evening's festivities. I rounded up the servants, ordered as sumptuous a meal as I could on short notice, and treated everyone as if royalty had arrived on my doorstep. His followers were disgruntled, but they had come along, taking Him at His word, astounded at His choice to visit my residence. I believe that Jesus acted in such a shockingly gracious manner so as to cause all of us to stop and think. He had this way of bringing everything down to the basics of life, to how we relate to each other in spite of our differences.

No one treated me the same after that night. I have never felt the same since, never seen myself as the same, small person—to be ignored or despised. This Nazarene, the Christ, gave me bigger shoes to fill, a larger burden to carry for others, and a sense of pride and gratitude.

He told a story shortly after visiting with me about a master who gave several servants the same amount of money to manage. The master then left the men to invest their wealth however they saw fit.

One increased his money ten times over. Another, five times. The last wrapped his up and hid it. The moral of the story I will never forget. Jesus said, "Risk your life and get more than you ever dreamed of. Play it safe and end up holding the bag."

From that day until my last, I made it a point to risk. To risk loving more, giving more, praying more, and being more of a man than ever before.

And the Nazarene—now my living Savior—was right. My life was full to overflowing. Not too bad for a little guy everybody thought was a nothing.

Jesus Understands

"Can anything make me stop loving you?" God asks. *"Watch me speak your language, sleep on your earth, and feel your hurts. Behold the maker of sight and sound as he sneezes, coughs, and blows his nose. You wonder if I understand how you feel? Look into the dancing eyes of the kid in Nazareth; that's God walking to school. Ponder the toddler at Mary's table; that's God spilling his milk."*

MAX LUCADO,
from *In the Grip of Grace*

Chapter Nineteen

THROW OUT THE FLANNELGRAPH!

Bonnie's Story

I'VE NEVER HAD A TASTE FOR KOOL-AID. Maybe it's because I subconsciously relate grape Kool-Aid to the muggy heat of summertime Vacation Bible School weeks at our church in the Deep South. At VBS, I made my share of pot holders for Mom and listened to stories told with flannelgraph characters while I dutifully drank my cup of sweet purple liquid.

The flannelgraph Bible characters never seemed real to me because they closely resembled my paper doll collection—my private, beloved stash. My paper-doll Flintstones and Barbies lined up comfortably next to the flannelgraph Moses in his cute little basket made of bulrushes—the one in which Miriam sent him floating down a storybook-blue Nile River.

These one-dimensional Bible-figure cutouts had no wrinkles, scars, or blemishes. The Jesus flannelgraph figure was happy and clean. I couldn't imagine these cutout Bible characters ever experiencing disappointment, or hunger, or sadness.

When I became an adult, life kicked me hard. For years, I was a single mom, divorced and scared to death. I needed a

God who was not a helpless cutout. I needed a God with skin on Him. I needed my Bible heroes to have flesh and blood and bone, to be real people that I could relate to. If I could identify with them in my loneliness and failures, then perhaps the Gospels I had studied all my life might hold up when everything else around me came crashing down.

Jesus...His flannelgraph figure looked so elusive and far away, so perfect, so removed from the messy, shaky, lonely place I found myself in. The faces of Christ I'd seen as a child and as an adult left me little room to believe that He could love me now—as messy, imperfect, and needy as I was.

It took my world's falling apart for me to comprehend the depth and width and humanity of Jesus' love. I threw out the flannelgraph images, the soulless figures of Christ, and went in search of God-yet-Man-yet-Messiah. I went looking for "new Kool-Aid"—for a release from my childhood preconceptions of God.

ONE OF THE FIRST THINGS I RECALL God giving me during a time of pleading, crying, questioning, and praying was this gentle nudging reminder: *Remember what Jesus said to the ones around Him who did not understand who He was. They railed against such a dusty, everyday man's man. He could not be the promised Savior! He didn't fit the suit, the image, the look, the plan they were counting on. He wasn't the Messiah He was supposed to be. My Son tried to explain this to them, saying, "You cannot put new wine into old wineskins!"* This thought took some studying for me to understand.

In biblical times, fasting was often a response to grief and mourning. When the Pharisees, who themselves fasted,

confronted Christ, they asked Him why He and His followers did not do the same. Jesus told them that His friends
were not sad, because He was with them! Jesus never beat
around the bush! He said, "People never pour new wine into
old leather bags. Otherwise, the bags will break, the wine will
spill, and the wine bags will be ruined. But people always
pour new wine into new wine bags. Then both will continue
to be good" (Matthew 9:17).

When I read this, I began to realize that Christ had to
become real to me. The old Kool-Aid-unapproachable-cutout
idea of Jesus had to be replaced with "new Kool-Aid."

Who is Jesus to you? What does He look like? Is He a
pale, waxy, untouchable face that gazes from the walls of
your childhood Sunday-school classroom? Is He real? Ap-
proachable? Is this kind of Jesus the reason you've never
darkened a church door?

Are you angry with Him, moved by Him, disturbed by
Him? Is He someone you might like to hang out with and
laugh and talk with? Or is He someone who would make
you uncomfortable with all His piety and perfection—a
flannelgraph figure?

In every way, Jesus was human and well-acquainted with
messy lives. He especially had a heart for fallen, shamed
women, and He sought them out in order to speak hope into
their disheveled lives. I finally realized He wasn't keeping me
at a distance—I was the one hiding from Him. The messages
I was sending myself about condemnation, disapproval, and
hopelessness were not from Jesus. He wasn't afraid of my
messy life—I was afraid of Him!

When I assumed that God couldn't love me anymore
because I was "messy," the old Kool-Aid was still running
through my veins. My self-righteous attitude turned inward,
and I became my own prosecutor, jury, and judge. I told myself

that God hated divorce, and therefore I was in for it. I convinced myself that God couldn't be around messy, worn-out, tired, lonely losers because He was unacquainted with messiness—just like the flannelgraph figure in my VBS lessons.

I was rewriting history. After all that Christ had endured to walk around like the rest of us—to be tired, weary, hungry, homeless, betrayed, angry, so very human to the core—was I going to be arrogant and presumptuous enough to believe that His sacrifices were not enough to cover the upheaval of my life?

Time for new wine—new Kool-Aid—time for a wake-up call as to how this Jesus was my brother and was still my Redeemer.

*   *   *

THE BOOK OF MATTHEW OPENS WITH the genealogy of Jesus. Philip Yancey observed, in *The Jesus I Never Knew*, that at first glance this long list of people seems unnecessary and perfunctory. Yet hidden here like undiscovered treasures are hints about how very human the Son of God would be. His lineage would never hold up to scrutiny at the blue-blood country clubs of our age. He would not have gained entry into any Ivy League university, and likely would have been turned away at the door of many a church.

He had a heritage of messy ancestors. For example, women were recorded in His genealogy, and this simply wasn't done in the Jewish cultural records of that time. And such unsavory women they were!

Tamar was a widow who had never borne children. Her name appears in the family tree of Jesus because she seduced her father-in-law in order to have a child—Judah.

Rahab, Boaz's mother, was a successful prostitute, who just happened to have a heart for God and His messengers in spite of her profession.

Bathsheba's adulterous relationship with David was the scandal of the day in the Old Testament, yet their second child, Solomon, was one of the wisest men of Israel.

Talk about some messed-up women! Yet God Almighty chose to come to Earth through this line of very human, very troubled women.

Writes Yancey, "These shady ancestors show that Jesus entered human history in the raw, a willing descendant of its shame. In contrast, Herod the Great, reigning king at Jesus' birth, had his genealogical records destroyed out of vanity because he wanted no one to compare his background with others'."

Throw out the sterile flannelgraph images of a weak, one-dimensional Jesus. The Jesus of the Gospels was a radical, passionate lover of the underdog. He stood the Jewish and Roman cultures on their heads.

Cee

IT ALL STARTS WITH THE CHRISTMAS STORY. Christmas is my favorite time of year, but I have to confess that, behind all the glitter and lights and pageants and "stuff," I struggle each year to remind myself of the dirt, the dark, the pain of a young teenage Mary and her nervous husband, Joseph. How in a cave, without help, they labored together and heard the first newborn cry—of God in the form of a helpless baby!

When we celebrate Christmas today, choirs sing, presents are exchanged, beautiful meals are created, and everything looks like it's coming up red and green. How often do we stop and think that the God of the universe chose to wrap Himself in human skin and become a human being? Isn't that what we are celebrating?

The meticulously arranged, candlelit services we hold on Christmas Eve attempt to remind us of this mystery. But the church has done a thorough job of sanitizing the coming of the Lord. He came to two poor teenagers in Nazareth, a city with a bad reputation. We forget the long journey on the back of a donkey to Bethlehem, the agony of Mary's labor, the lack of sterile conditions. His mother and father delivered Him together, much like someone caught on a back road, having run out of gas on the way to the hospital, the cell-phone battery dead.

God came to us as a baby, from a human womb, through the birth pangs of a tenderhearted teenager. He cut teeth. He may have had diaper rash—who knows? He had to learn to crawl, then pull Himself up and walk. He likely got sick, threw up, and ran fevers. Christ endured the rigorous passages of manhood. He went through adolescence, and maybe even had pimples.

Jesus did not insulate Himself from humanity.

He embraced it.

The brilliant mercy of God was predicted by Isaiah. He described the coming Messiah as a humble human being: "He grew up like a small plant before the LORD, like a root growing in a dry land. He had no special beauty or form to make us notice him; there was nothing in his appearance to make us desire him" (Isaiah 53:2). Jesus entered the world, lived life, and ended it as we do: in painful, messy difficulty.

This was a Jesus I could confidently trust in my deepest hours of depression. I tasted new Kool-Aid—and it was great! I found hope in the midst of upheaval. I began to love Him. I found a Savior who blessed the weak, the poor in spirit, the needy, the humble, and the shaky—others like me. Jesus let me know He was here for me, He understood my circumstances. He had overcome this world so I could hold on to Him and become a survivor—through His strength!

If God had chosen any other path, I would have no reason to believe that He loves me in spite of divorce, brokenhearted seasons of bitterness and anger, fear of the future, and loneliness of spirit. But God has come to me "with skin on Him" as Jesus. He is no cutout, no one-dimensional flannelgraph figure. He is my Jesus, the Son of Man and the seed of the woman, a person and a God who relates to me and is ever-present. He's as close as my next breath, beside me in depression and defeat, beside me cheering me on in the good times.

Unless Jesus is real to you, in all His humanity, the great gift of His divinity will never cut through your circumstances and pierce your heart. Being a mess is in your bloodline. He knows that. Knew it before you were born. But He came to deliver you *from* the messiness of this world. He'll meet you in the direst of places, when you least believe you're not worth meeting at all.

Let Him in.

Flesh Him out.

Walk with Him.

Spill out your heart to Him.

Laugh and cry with Him.

Then worship at His feet.

*A*ll those who stand before others and say they believe in me, I will say before my Father in heaven that they belong to me...Don't think that I came to bring peace to the earth. I did not come to bring peace, but a sword. I have come so that "a son will be against his father, a daughter will be against her mother...a person's enemies will be members of his own family."

JESUS,
in Matthew 10:32-36.
(He is quoting Micah 7:6.)

Chapter Twenty

HOW WILL I THANK HIM?

Parwin's Story

WHERE WOULD MY LIFE BE WITHOUT my family? My family loves the Lord, and from the cradle, they pointed me in the direction of Jesus so I could know more of His love. My parents are warm, supportive, salt-of-the-earth people. They have helped me raise my two children, and they saw me through the hardest years when I was divorced and a single parent. Without their support and encouragement, I don't know how I could have continued to minister, work, and take care of Courtney and Graham. All that is good in my life has come from the hard work of my father, the creative passion of my mother, and the joy of having terrific siblings in Amy and Stan. At every messy step of my life I have found their arms open wide to hold me up and show me unconditional love.

I didn't truly understand the words of Matthew 10—see the opposite page—until I met Parwin Moore. When she told me bits and pieces of her life story, I was dumbfounded by all she had endured. Parwin had tears in her eyes as she spoke to me about her family and told me of the price she's paid for her faith in Christ. "He knew—Jesus knew these things would happen when He said those words," Parwin told me. "He knows just how I feel."

Upon meeting Parwin, the first thing that struck me was her startling beauty—flashing brown-black eyes set in a classic face that's surrounded by thick, raven-black hair. But more striking than her physical attractiveness is Parwin's spirit, which radiates joy. Parwin and her husband, Ron, had recently been married, and so at first I chalked up Parwin's glow to the "honeymoon syndrome." Since Ron and I were scheduled to share ministry time at a church in Oklahoma City, I took the opportunity to get to know Parwin better. Her glow, I quickly discovered, comes from a heart filled with a passionate love for God, a kind of love that I've rarely seen up close.

Cee

PARWIN IS A NATIVE OF AFGHANISTAN. Her father was one of the royal political figures who served Muhammad Zahir Shah, the former king, who was ousted in 1973. Parwin's family was large, with ten children, and an entourage of maids, cooks, and staff took care of their every need. Her father was wealthy and well-respected and loved his family more than life itself.

The Afghanistan of Parwin's childhood was quite a bit different than the one Americans now see on the news. Parwin said her country formerly was a place where women went to universities, and the large cities were clean and modern. But this would soon change. When the king was exiled, Parwin's father saw the dangers to him and his family that were posed by the newly formed government. By the time her family fled, the strongest and best men were being killed in the long conflict that had started, and like a deadly virus, the new regime began to change the entire tone of the country.

"By now, there are mostly women, children, old people, and many suffering ones left," Parwin reflected sadly. "So many others have died and been killed."

Parwin's father sent his children—one by one—to the United States, where they would be safe. Parwin was sent to live with friends and relatives, eventually ending up in Oklahoma. Her father stubbornly stayed in Afghanistan, trying to find a way for his youngest daughter and her husband to leave the country. As a result, he was placed under house arrest by the Russian invaders, suffering beatings and other mistreatments. This continued even after his daughter and her husband were able to flee. Finally, Parwin's father and mother were also able to escape to America, and the family was reunited.

Parwin soon married a suitor who had followed her from Afghanistan to the United States. Her marriage quickly turned into a nightmare. Her husband treated her disrespectfully, as more of a decorative accessory than a person. Parwin was expected to accompany him to his many business appearances, country-club events, and social activities. She remembers her husband telling her, "You're nothing to me but a pretty face."

Parwin's self-esteem was soon destroyed. Emotionally she was beaten to a pulp. She was mistreated by her husband, threatened, and kept in a prison of fear. But her culture gave her no option of leaving this man. Soon Parwin was a walking corpse, a mannequin devoid of all emotion. She was told what to wear, where to go, and what to say. If she did not behave as her husband liked, he brutally abused her. She, and soon her two daughters, endured this cruelty in surroundings of opulence and material possessions. But although things were in order outwardly, her life was a catastrophic mess.

"I had a Mercedes parked in the garage, a huge home, two little girls, a husband who was making more money than he could spend—and I was a broken human being," Parwin remembers. "I was terrified for anyone to know, because he told me if I ever left he would kill both me and our daughters."

Parwin's daughters begged their mother to let them attend a local youth group gathering with Christian friends from school. She finally relented and let them go. During their time at these meetings, her daughters became Christians, and they began to pray for their mother. Terrified, Parwin hid the girls' conversion from her husband and chalked up their newfound faith to a "phase" that teenagers go through.

⁓

As Parwin's life became more and more unbearable, she knew that, if she were to survive, she had to find a way to Allah, the God she had been taught about as a child. Although she had grown up in a Muslim country, she knew little about Allah. But she was determined to find a source of strength. So Parwin did something that Muslims rarely do— especially Muslim women. She read the Quran, the Muslims' holy book, six times in its entirety. Each time she read it, she became more and more confused by the teachings. Husbands were told that they had the right to punish their wives; they were allowed, according to the Quran, to have as many as four wives. Although polygamy is not generally encouraged by Muslim thinkers, Parwin read with dismay about the great prophet Muhammad, who took more than ten wives, one of them a nine-year-old girl.

Worst of all, Parwin found Allah to be a frightening God—difficult to love, impossible to connect with. She was full of questions, and wanted desperately to find a path to God so that she could survive her pressure-cooker marriage. Why were men taught to hurt their wives if they felt it was justified? How did one experience love from Allah? Frustration drove her to seek out clerics at a local mosque so she could ask them for help in understanding Allah. And she wanted answers to the gnawing question she had about how Muhammad could be such a holy figure when he was having sex with a child.

Much to her dismay, the clerics told her that they would not speak to her about Muhammad. They silenced her and sent her away.

Parwin continued her life of fear. Her husband and his brother openly spoke of simply slitting her throat if she didn't "behave." When she finally found the courage to leave her husband, he put out a contract for her murder.

Panicked, Parwin called the police, begging them to believe what sounded like a ridiculous story. She was relieved when the police believed her, after learning that her husband was of the Muslim faith. They told her that several Muslim wives had been in similar situations—and a restraining order was placed on her husband, which is still in effect today.

Frightened, lonely, and sick to the core of her soul, Parwin yearned to know God. One day, she noticed a Bible in her daughter's room. She picked it up and began to read. How amazed she was to find that Jesus was so young when He was killed—and that He had been crucified like a thief.

Parwin had been told that He was a prophet who had died of old age. As she read, Parwin was enthralled with the Jesus she discovered. She fell in love with His mercy and grace. She was flooded with joy when she realized that she could pray directly to God, the God of the Bible, and that He wanted her to talk with Him. Though she'd been taught never to cry, was told it was a disgrace, years of tears began to flow from her wounded spirit, and she began to be healed.

HER NEW LIFE CAME AT A TREMENDOUS COST.

Parwin's mother demanded that she return to her husband. When she refused, and then told her mother of her daughters' and her own new faith, her mother was horrified. Parwin became officially dead to her family, who held a funeral for her and her two girls. No one in the family was to have contact with them.

Parwin was her father's favorite daughter, however, and she held him in great love and respect. On his deathbed, she was with him. He was not a practicing Muslim, and he allowed Parwin to hold him in her arms and rock him back and forth, as he had rocked her so lovingly when she was ill as a child. She wanted so much for him to know the Jesus she had discovered. She prayed for his salvation. Was it too late?

The last words he said to Parwin came to her like manna from heaven. "I know the truth. I know the truth. I know the truth," he told her. And then he died.

Both of Parwin's fathers saved her life. Her self-esteem now comes from knowing she is a daughter, not only of an earthly father, but of an all-loving, all-seeing heavenly

Father. Her life has radically changed because of the love of Jesus.

She doesn't complain when she speaks of the funeral her mother held for her. But when she tells me she wonders if she will ever see her sisters and brothers again, her eyes fill with tears.

"Jesus came for people like me, to families like mine, where some would hate Him and others would find life in Him," Parwin said. "My mother hates me because I love Christ. My sisters and brothers are forbidden to see me or speak to me. I may never see any of them again."

Then, right after these agony-filled words, like a little child Parwin threw her arms wide—just as if it were Christmas morning and she'd just opened the most wonderful gift under the tree. "Jesus is why I am alive today! My family believes I am dead, but they don't know how very alive I am! Without Christ I would not be here. I was dead before...I was going to be killed and my spirit was so lonely, so heavy, so sad...Oh, I love Jesus so! I think about this all the time...What will I say when I see Him, Bonnie? I don't know what I'll do! What will I do when He's right there in front of me?"

I, for one, cannot wait to see that embrace.

When the fulness of the time was come, God sent forth his Son, made of a woman, made under the law, to redeem them that were under the law, that we might receive the adoption of sons. And because ye are sons, God hath sent forth the Spirit of his Son into your hearts, crying, Abba, Father. Wherefore thou art no more a servant, but a son; and if a son, then an heir of God through Christ.

GALATIANS 4:4-7 (KJV)

Chapter Twenty-One

JUST SAY THE WORD

The Roman Soldier

NEWS OF JESUS' GREAT WISDOM *and ability to heal both physical and mental torment spread throughout Israel during His
three-year ministry. Although many of His own people refused
to accept Him despite the miracles He performed each day, for
others it was more simple.*

*A Roman officer who watched the ministry of Jesus unfold
somehow became filled with a childlike faith in Him. When a
loved servant became ill, the Roman officer believed that Jesus,
the miracle-worker, could heal him. Although it put him at
risk—going to Jesus publicly—the Roman officer laid aside his
own concern and boldly asked Jesus for help.*

*Jesus, never one to remain unmoved by a heart of faith, and
endlessly open to rearranging His schedule, agreed to go with the
man to his home. Imagine the murmurs of disapproval that
arose from those around Him at the thought of Jesus entering
the house of a despised Roman officer—an unclean Gentile!
Here's what the situation might have looked like from the
Roman officer's point of view…*

I HAD SEEN MANY PROPHETS come through Israel during my service as a Roman official in the region of Capernaum. Whenever another holy man gained prominence, we were told to be on guard against any uprisings and violence, especially from the Zealots, who jumped on any chance to fight the Romans in the name of their God.

So when Jesus of Nazareth began to teach, I and my men would go and stand close by to keep the peace. We were attentive in case the gathering crowd became unruly. It was during these hours of watch that the words of Jesus began to soften my heart.

Everything about Him was different from anything I had seen before. John the Baptist, Jesus' predecessor, was full of wrath and radical calls for repentance. He met his end in a prison, beheaded by Herod. Jesus was the cousin of John, and I expected to hear the same passionate entreaties for repentance in Jesus' preaching.

Yet when Jesus spoke, His words were full of compassion, grace, forgiveness, and mercy. He spoke of loving your enemy, doing good to those who treat you badly, paying taxes to the Romans as they were due, and becoming born again by following and believing in Him.

The Jews—oh, how they hated me! They would glare at me as I stood on the fringes of the crowd, their eyes full of resentment and fear. In them I saw the terrible pain of a people relentlessly beaten down by our government.

I did not enjoy having to command that certain laws be carried out. But I was proud of my position, and my men were proud to serve under me. I treated them well, and all in my household were regarded with respect, even my servants.

In truth, one of my servants was one of the best men I have ever known. When he became gravely ill, I knew I had to find Jesus to ask for help. I had seen Jesus heal many,

many people. Blind people. Deaf people. Outcasts with leprosy. Almost in a panic, I went searching for Him so He could heal my servant.

I found Jesus as He was coming down from the mountains and approaching Capernaum. The crowds following Him that day were cheering, and I screwed up my courage and made my way toward Him. There wasn't much time. My servant was dying, and I didn't know if he would live through the night.

"Master," I said to Jesus, "my servant is sick. He cannot walk. He is in terrible pain!"

The eyes of the Prophet met mine. The men around Him fell silent. Disapproval hung in the air. Would Jesus dismiss me?

I stood before Him, the very symbol of the oppression and persecution of His people. But Jesus seemed to see me, not my uniform. He looked at me without anger. Quietly, He told me He would come to my house.

"No," I said to Him, stopping Him with a gesture, "I don't want to put You to all of that trouble. I know that it would not be right for You to enter my home. But I do know this— just give the order, and I know my servant will be well. I am a man who takes and gives orders. I know that if I order one of the men in my service to go, he will go. Or if I order another to come, he will come. So I know too that You have the power to send the illness from the body of my servant, if only You will say the word."

I looked at Jesus, who stood with a look of amazement on His face. He turned to His disciples and spoke. "I have yet to come across this kind of simple trust in Israel, among the very ones who have been taught to know all about Jehovah God and how He works. This man, a Roman, is the vanguard, the first of many outsiders who will soon be coming to Me from all the earth—streaming in from the east, pouring in from the west, sitting down together at God's kingdom feast along with Abraham, Isaac, and Jacob."

Oh! The Jews did not like His words. They began to murmur angrily, and some looked at me in disgust. But a few of His disciples smiled at me, and the one named John looked at me encouragingly, full in the face.

Then Jesus said, "Those who grow up 'in the faith' but have little faith will find themselves left out in the cold. They will be outsiders to grace and wonder what has happened to them." Then Jesus touched me on my shoulder.

"Go home," He told me. "What you believed could happen, has happened."

I fell to my knees in gratitude, then the crowd slowly parted as I quickly turned and sped for home. I was still a little ways off when my family rushed out to meet me with the news. The very hour Jesus had spoken, my servant had been healed!

I continued to listen to Jesus and began to believe that He was the "Son of Man" and the Son of the Hebrew God. Committing His words to memory, I pondered all He said and asked questions—of those who would answer—about how Jesus' life compared with the prophecies in the Jewish Scriptures.

Even after I and my troops were moved to Jerusalem, the capital of Judea, I continued to ask news of Jesus. When He came to the city, I hoped I might have more opportunities to listen to His words.

But He was arrested and condemned to be crucified. My men were on call to stand guard over Him at the hill of Golgotha. I was there, though not in uniform. Standing in the rain, watching Him die, my servant and I wept with disbelief that such a kind, good, loving, and healing Prophet could suffer such a cruel ending.

Three days later, I heard the news of how the body of Jesus was missing from the tomb. I couldn't help but smile at the chaos His empty tomb created. Of course He was gone. No tomb could hold this Jesus. Not even death itself had power over Him. To rise again, all He had to do was to say the word.

Grace from the Heart of God

My doubts spring from the depths of my own inferiority. If I detect these misgivings in myself, I should bring them into the light and confess them openly—"Lord, I have had misgivings about you. I have not believed in Your abilities but only in my own. And I have not believed in Your Almighty power apart from my own finite understanding of it."

OSWALD CHAMBERS,
from *My Utmost for His Highest*

Chapter Twenty-Two

SPEAKING THE UNSPEAKABLE

Bonnie's Story

THE ROOM BECAME DEATHLY QUIET. I had been speaking to a large singles' gathering, telling them about my near date-rape experience. I thought to myself, *Well, you've finally gone over the edge here. What are you doing? No one wants to hear about this, and how in the world can you segue into a song or a light anecdote now?* Despite feeling as if I'd put my foot squarely in my mouth, I continued to describe the horrible night I had spent wrestling down a friend—a would-be date. Finally, I told the gathering how I'd talked this man into leaving my home before I ended up either completely violated or cut up into little pieces and buried under my front porch.

"I've shared this with you tonight in hopes that some of you might avoid this dating land mine by learning from my mistakes," I said confidently, despite my pounding heart.

After the concert I sat down at the table where my books and CDs were being sold so I could talk with whoever might want to say hello. To my astonishment, the first three women who came to talk with me were all date-rape victims.

One of them told me how she had become pregnant with her attacker's child, yet had chosen to keep the baby. Each of the three was in tears as she shared her story with me, each finding solace in the fact that I also was a survivor of the shame that such an experience inflicts.

One woman held on to me, weeping, and said, "No one ever talks about this in church. I've never felt like I could let it go until now. Thank you." So much for the foot in the mouth. Maybe that's where it belongs!

When I tell my story to listeners around the country, I sense an immediate connection. I hear story after story from hurting, bleeding people who are carrying around the very burdens Christ died to free them from. Ironically, it appears that the church has something to do with this.

Fear affects all of us in different ways, and it's my theory that fear of the unknown keeps the church from knowing how to deal with the unspeakable pain of the people sitting in the pews. We're fearful of not knowing what to say, fearful of being offended, fearful of our own private demons. Fear—in all kinds of disguises—keeps many members of the church from reaching out to the bleeding people around them.

There are many ways for the church to reach out to those with messy lives. Everywhere I speak, I ask local churches to consider starting a ministry to the single parents in their body—even just a fund for grocery money or for bills that cannot be paid. I also speak of the need for men and women to be willing to spend time with young boys or girls who need strong, loving role models in their lives. In my home church, we have a ministry called "The Samaritan Purse," and the staff is encouraged to make sure all of the money in the fund is spent by the end of each year in helping families. There are so many ways to reach out! And most often, hurting people are looking for someone to listen, to hold them, to forgive them, and to embrace them without judgment.

Clee

IN MY ROLE AS A "POSTER CHILD" for problems, I've also been surprised by the number of men and women who have called or written to tell me they are fellow sufferers from depression. The Bible devotes many passages to the messiness of depression. The feeling of being left alone, of being on the edge of utter despair, is a human condition common to many people of faith.

Speaking about this unmentionable phenomenon has been a challenge for me. As a person of deep faith, I still continue to battle depression. It is not a mark of my personality or a result of my belief system. Rather, depression is a part of my emotional-chemical makeup. If God allowed a miracle of healing in me, I would gratefully, ecstatically embrace it.

Until that happens, I take my medications, and I read the Word and study to stay centered on the Lord, knowing that I tend to fall into overwhelming sadness when I allow either my schedule or my personal life to get out of order. Intense emotional times—sad or joyful—can catch me off balance. Reluctantly, I have come to realize that I quite easily fall prey to too much input, stress, change, or pressure. I cave in. I cannot "roll with it, baby" like some others I know. This is just how I am wired. And it's taken me years—and ongoing conversations with my godly, wonderful doctor—to accept this about myself. Depression seems shameful. But it's a condition I cannot deny.

I wish I could count the number of people who have contacted me about their own battle with depression. Far too many of these people are afraid to tell anyone at their home church about their pain, fearing that they will be chastised or looked down upon. This is wrong! It needs to change!

There are record numbers of people in this country that are suffering from depression. In our country and our culture, as our pace of living increases to a ridiculous speed, as our intake of information bombards us with losses and pain that we have no place to put, the incidence of depression increases. Add to this personal struggles with divorce, single loneliness, single parenthood, financial pressure, and a myriad of other problems, and you have an American Christian culture that is not insulated from the world's sadness and suffering.

We all live on a fallen, hurting planet. We all have to survive our circumstances as best we can, relying on the grace of Christ and the mercy of God. Yet some of us are not as strong as others.

I beseech all Christians to be kind to and open to those who suffer from the unspeakable affliction of depression. It could be your neighbor, your spouse, or your best friend who is afraid to confess that their life is not worth living. Despite their deep convictions and commitment to Christ, this world is spinning too fast, is too out of control, for far too many people of faith.

There are answers.

There is treatment.

There are medications, simple and gentle, and they can be temporary for many who need to simply get physical rest and get back to a starting point. They aren't necessarily needed for a long period of time. I think of such medical assistance as the same as the help one gets from antibiotics to cure an infection. After one's body is stronger and back to normal, the antibiotics have done their work. The same is true for many antidepressants. For a great number of suffering people, a short time of medication would act to bring their season of emotional exhaustion to an end.

The Scriptures are filled with passages that honor and respect this human condition. Most powerful for me is the picture of Christ in Gethsemane: "Being full of pain, Jesus prayed even harder. His sweat was like drops of blood falling to the ground" (John 22:44).

I hope pastors and counselors will invite those who are silently suffering with depression to come forward so they can be met with grace and nonjudgmental responses. If the church is to be effective in this turn of the millennium culture, we must open our eyes and address the subject. The increase in the number of people filled with grief, thirsty for help, is staggering. More than six million people in America alone deal with some form of this disease. For many, it is an unmentionable condition of the heart and soul, one that is swept under the rug of pious disrespect and ignorance. Yet nothing, not even the imprisonment of a human spirit in the abysmal darkness of despair, is beyond Christ's touch.

If the church is the heart and body of Christ—His hands and arms, eyes and ears—then it must take off the blinders, become informed, and reach out to the growing number of people who are literally dying for help. Christ knows well how they feel. He will give relief to all who knock on His door, no matter how weak they are when they arrive there.

We must not be afraid to speak of the unspeakable. For with the love of our Jesus, fear is cast out, and there is nothing that cannot be addressed and healed by the power of His blood. Those of us who are strong must reach out to those who are faint of heart and spirit. We are called to be the body of Jesus fearlessly—to fearlessly be the Son of Man to each other. I beg all of us to move beyond our fear of depression, to open our hearts to speak—to the broken jars of clay, the paralyzed of spirit—this truth:

> *We have treasures from God, but we are like clay jars that hold the treasure. This shows that the great power is from God, not from us. We have troubles all around us, but we are not defeated. We do not know what to do, but we do not give up hope of living. We are persecuted but God does not leave us. We carry the death of Jesus in our bodies so that the life of Jesus can also be seen in our bodies. So we do not give up. Our physical body is becoming older and weaker, but our spirit inside us is made new every day. We have small troubles for a while now, but they are helping us gain an eternal glory that is greater than the troubles. We set our eyes not on what we see but on what we cannot see. What we see will last only a short time, but what we cannot see will last forever (2 Corinthians 3:7-9,16-18).*

Love bears up under anything and *everything that comes, is ever ready to believe the best of every person, its hopes are fadeless under all circumstances, and it endures everything [without weakening]. Love never fails.*

1 CORINTHIANS 13:7 (AMP)

CROSSING THE RIVER

Steve's Story

No matter what our battle is with—fear, depression, shame—we must cross the river of suffering and come to the other side, either bitter—or stronger.

Steve is a brilliant person and was gifted in a highly specialized field of medicine. He pioneered some of the most advanced technology that is used in surgery today. His work took him to hospitals and to top surgical teams from Utah to Pittsburgh. He finally ended up working with the best of the best.

For those of you who, like me, have a hard time understanding even the simplest of processes, I'll describe Steve's specialty this way. The device he developed was the one adopted to rapidly deliver a large amount of blood in a short time—such as is needed during transplant surgery or when treating major injuries. He had no formal training for this work, but he was miraculously gifted with technical and manual skill and was put in a position so wonderful that it took his breath away. He relished the chance to work with and gain the respect of elite doctors in this field. In no time at all, Steve was on the fast track.

Steve is a husband and father, and he's quick to pull out the pictures from his wallet and proudly show off his beautiful family. But his marriage was messy, as many are, and there were times when he and his wife faced separation and divorce.

Steve takes much of the blame for their problems. He admits to having been arrogant, rocking along the road of good fortune—life in the fast lane. He took the precious people in his life for granted. Perhaps being so swiftly caught up into such an impressive line of work went to his head. And despite the complexity of his job, understanding his role at work was easier than understanding his role as a husband and father.

However, Steve had given his life to Jesus long before his life hit the messy part. The Jesus he knew, the Spirit of God that he had accepted years earlier, began to gently, relentlessly speak to him. Steve told me how he became convinced that true love is not to be denied—the love of God, that is. If he was to love his wife as God's love instructed him, then he had to see the vows he'd taken as holy and sacred, ones to be honored.

"The Bible says that love hopes, endures, and bears all things. Love never fails. As I reflected back to when we were first married, I knew beyond a shadow of a doubt that I had loved my wife then. I came to the point where I had to decide—either the Bible was a lie, or it was *I* who had failed.

"That chapter in Corinthians about love weighed on my conscience, and I couldn't stand to disgrace God's love and the love for my wife that I was called to. There were false gods in my life I had been putting before my wife. I confessed these things to her and walked away from the Ishmaels in my world."

This was a horrid, difficult, painful choice. His wife, to her credit, accepted the tender coming-clean experience with Steve, and they moved forward with their marriage. Steve was working hard to prove to himself, his wife, and the Lord that he could live a life of renewed integrity. With a spirit of courage, he tried to do each next right thing. "As my best friend often says to me, 'I wish doing the right thing felt better. Shouldn't we get some kind of payoff, win a lottery or something, when we choose the right path?' At times doing the next right thing feels so bad, but you have to go ahead— knowing that feelings aren't always reality."

Slowly Steve's marriage became stronger, and their lives gained a closer intimacy and trust. Then one day, he went by his brother's house and decided he'd ride his brother's motorcycle just for fun. He called his wife to see if she had any reservations, telling himself that if she didn't want him to, then he wouldn't take the drive. As bad timing—or God's timing—would have it, she had just stepped out of the house for a few moments to take their toddler son for a walk, and she missed his call. So, thinking it would only be a short ride and not much of a risk, off he went. A few, short minutes later, his life changed forever.

Steve was approaching one of Pittsburgh's beautiful bridges, traveling about 30 miles an hour, when everything went wrong. He took the bend too wide. As he straightened up on the bike, his right shoulder hit the first girder on the bridge. The side of his head then struck the second girder, and he was thrown into the middle of the roadway. As he lay there looking up at the sky, with cars quickly bearing down on him, he realized he could feel nothing from his neck down. "If I have to live paralyzed, dear Lord, please let me die right now," he prayed.

As the ambulance arrived, at that very moment pain seared through his arms and shoulders. One of the bitter ironies of Steve's crucible of suffering is that, with all the great surgeons at his disposal, he was sent to a hospital where he had not worked. Struggling to have someone believe him, he tried desperately to convey to the medical staff what was happening in his body. But no one would listen to him, and in the end, he was given a wrong diagnosis based on someone else's X rays. By the time he finally got through to a doctor at his home hospital and was transferred, the use of his arm was lost…the arm that had allowed him to help so many others.

Steve continues to struggle with the results of his ride on that sunny day in July. With gratitude in his voice, he thanks God that his family continues to grow (he now has two lovely daughters as well as a son), and that he and his wife are doing well. But the medical community in Steve's world turned their backs on him. In an act of horrendous timing, only hours after learning he would never use his arm again, he was informed that he would no longer have a job. He received almost no financial help despite his years of hard work and service to develop groundbreaking technology. Steve found out who his true friends were the hard way.

Yet the most awesome thing about this man is the light in his eyes. He's "contending," as he calls it, with his situation. He's wrestling God's angels down one by one—with his one, very strong arm. He now works with a Christian television company and does whatever he's asked to do. He learns, drinks in every word of Scripture and encouragement, and believes that God has more for him on the other side of his bridge.

Steve drove me around Pittsburgh when I was there on a promotional tour. When I jumped into the car so he could take me to the television studio, he launched into a series of questions about my life, my faith, and the messiness I'd seen. Without missing a beat, he matter of factly asked, "So, how did you cross the river?"

What a terrific way to put it. How do each of us respond to this crazy world and what comes roaring in? I realized we all have those bridges, those moments where life dips and turns and we lose things that are precious. I determined that Steve had much to teach me. I wanted to ask him a thousand questions, but he seemed even more eager to hear my story, perhaps to find in it a nugget of encouragement that I might offer him in his journey.

Before I left Pittsburgh, among other gifts, Steve gave me a rock that I noticed he kept in the dashboard of his car—a rock he'd taken from the river near the place he'd had his accident. "You mustn't give this to me!" I said, nearly crying.

"I want you to have it!" he laughed. "There are dozens of those rocks, and I can get another one anytime."

There are dozens of rocks, that's true, dozens of reminders of the hard places life takes us. Trusting God to use these seemingly unbearable experiences for good is what our faith all boils down to. I saw that kind of stubborn trust in Steve's life and face and laugh, and in his hunger to know God more deeply.

And his gift now goes with me in my travel bag. It's a reminder that we all cross rivers, and some of us hit the bridge…But as Steve's faith reminded me, how we cross the river is up to each of us. The rivers, the bridges can save our lives; they can change us if we let them. Our losses can leave us cold and bitter. Or we can wear our scars as proof that God will meet us when we have to go in the water, will give us the grace that will take us to the other side.

[Jesus] would let himself get distracted by any "nobody" he came across, whether a hemorrhaging woman…a blind beggar…

PHILIP YANCEY,
from *The Jesus I Never Knew*

Chapter Twenty-Four

THE WRONG MAN FOR THE RIGHT JOB

Moses

MOSES WAS A MAN BORN A HEBREW *and raised as Egyptian roy-alty, only to be banished from Egypt when he discovered his true heritage and murdered an Egyptian who was mistreating one of his countrymen. Then, 40 years later, God sent him back to Egypt to rescue the Hebrew people. I can never hear this story without thinking of the movie* The Ten Commandments. *When I watched it as a child, I was always left with my mouth hanging open as I watched Moses (Charlton Heston) spread his arms over the Red Sea, the waters parting so the Israelites could walk through "on dry land" to escape the Egyptian army.*

AT THE TIME OF MOSES' BIRTH, *the pharaoh of Egypt had decreed that all male Hebrew babies be killed. Moses' mother made a basket for her baby son and sent her daughter Miriam to place it on the waters of the River Nile and watch over it. Miriam reported that a miracle had occurred. The princess of Egypt, while bathing with her entourage in the river, had found the baby Moses and decided to adopt him as her own.*

For many years Moses grew in strength. He became a man well-respected among the people of Egypt. All the while, the

Hebrew nation—Moses' true people—was enslaved to the pharaoh. For more than 300 years their prayers had gone up to God, asking Him to free them from their bondage.

Moses was out watching one day as the Hebrews were being mistreated. Moved by their burdens, he decided to take matters into his own hands. Believing that no one was watching, Moses slew one of the Egyptians who was beating one of the Hebrews. He hid the dead man's body in the sand.

The next day, however, he was confronted by two Hebrew men who were quarreling. When Moses asked them why they were fighting among themselves, they returned the same question to him: "Why did you kill one of your own?"

Pharaoh heard of the murder, and Moses, fearing for his life, left Egypt and took refuge in the land of Midian. There he took a wife, Zipporah, and began a new life, fathering a son named Gershom. He tended flocks of sheep for his father-in-law—until one fateful day.

In the 40 years since Moses had left Egypt, the king he had known had died. Yet the people of Israel remained in bondage, crying out even more intensely to God for deliverance. And the Lord heard their sighing and groaning and remembered His covenant with Abraham, Isaac, and Jacob. And He thought of Moses...

I'VE NEVER BEEN GREAT WITH BIG WORDS or fancy sentences. I get ahead of myself, and usually what I mean to say comes out the wrong way, gets twisted around. Growing up in Egypt, I didn't have to rely on my speaking skills to get by. I had a big enough heart, and I was raised by the princess herself. It wasn't until many years into my adulthood that I realized that I was a Hebrew, a blood brother of the slaves we used to do the backbreaking work of building temples to the Egyptian gods, and pyramids for the pharaohs.

Too many times I saw my brothers beaten and abused by the Egyptian guards who stood over them with whips in their hands. I was hotheaded. Quick to anger. Too quick to act before I thought. One day, I'd had enough. I killed an Egyptian who deserved to die and buried him in the sand nearby. I hadn't seen anyone looking, and thought I was free and clear. But the pharaoh found out, and I was terrified of what might happen to me.

A fine mess I'd made of my life with one irrational move. Nothing would ever be the same for me in Egypt, so I ran as far away as I could. I ended up in the land of Midian, where I started a new life.

I married, and soon my wife and I were blessed with a son. Working for my father-in-law gave me contentment I had not known in Egypt. I had left behind my troubles and was at peace. However, God had other plans for me. There I was, minding my own business, quietly living my life...when I saw a burning bush!

I was out near Mount Sinai, moving my flocks, when I saw the flames. The bush seemed to be completely on fire, yet it wasn't burned up. Curious, I moved closer.

My heart jumped into my throat when a voice spoke to me out of the bush. *Yahweh* told me that I was the one He had chosen to go to Egypt and deliver His people from bondage! God was speaking to *me*?

For 40 years I had been rid of Egypt and glad of it. There were many days when my life there seemed like a distant dream, something that had happened to someone else. But God announced that He was sending me back and asking me to do an impossible task. I was to free His people. My body shook with fear. Surely, God must have set the bush on fire in front of the wrong man!

I fell to the ground, trembling so hard my teeth were chattering. "No, God, not me! I know You're God, but You must have the wrong guy. I stutter, I'm not a great speaker—in fact, I am slow to find the right words, and now, even talking with *You*, I can't pull a sentence together. I'm not big on crowds! Your people won't believe You sent me! How will I win their trust? How in the world will I know what to say? Haven't You thought about my brother, Aaron—now *he* could pull this off…"

Finally, after He had answered every one of my fearful objections with His promises to give me all I needed, after He had said things like, "I AM that I AM," I believed He was starting to lose His almighty temper with me. "Who made a person's mouth? Who makes someone deaf or not able to speak? Or gives sight or blindness? It is I, the Lord. Now go! I will help you speak, and I will teach you what to say," said the Lord. And He did indeed do that very thing.

Quaking in my boots, off I went to do the Lord's will. I felt like the worst, most ill-equipped man in the world for this job.

Doesn't God use the most unlikely people to do His work?

THE STORY OF MOSES IS THE VERY HUMAN *story of all who are spoken to—in whatever way, great or small—out of the burning bushes in our lives. Those places where the Lord speaks our name and asks us to be His hands and feet and light and deliverance for a dying world.*

In the messy, awkward, reluctant life of this servant, God once again used a person's willingness to step out—even in fear—to accomplish His miracle of freedom.

I was absolutely thunderstruck by the extraordinary reality of the man I found in the Gospels (Christ). I discovered a man who was almost continually frustrated…a man who was frequently sad and sometimes depressed, frequently anxious and scared…a man who was terribly, terribly lonely, yet often desperately needed to be alone. I discovered a man so incredibly real that no one could have made Him up.

SCOTT PECK,
from *Further Along the Road Less Traveled*

EPILOGUE

The Messy Life of Jesus

He who is the Bread of Life began His ministry hungering.
He who is the Water of Life ended His ministry thirsting.
Christ hungered as a man, yet fed the hungry as God.
He was weary, yet He is our rest.
He paid tribute, yet He is the King.
He was called a devil, but He cast out demons.
He prayed, and He hears prayer.
He wept, and He dries our tears.
He was sold for 30 pieces of silver, yet He redeems sinners.
He was led as a lamb to the slaughter, yet He is the
   Good Shepherd.
He gave His life, and by dying, He destroyed death.

ANONYMOUS

THE SINLESS LIFE OF JESUS SCARES many of us away. If I am aware of my imperfection, how can I relate to a perfect Jesus without overwhelming guilt and shame? The human perfection of Jesus was a sign of His divinity. He said that He and the Father were as One, and that He could do nothing apart from the strength of God. Are any of us able to say the same?

227

Does God expect perfection? No! Jesus knew we would fail. We cannot be what He was. Yet, through His blood, we are seen by the Father as righteous. God's love for us is preposterous, outrageous!

For the very moments you feel there is no hope, Jesus came to give you hope! The only way He could accomplish this was to taste life Himself. How could He be in tune with grief and suffering if He hadn't put His heart out on the line and found Himself rejected?

In *Reflections for Ragamuffins,* Brennan Manning writes,

> *When God drew aside the curtain of eternity and stepped into human history in the man of Jesus, he fully assumed the human condition down to the last joyful or painful experience. The Word was made flesh. He was really one of us. Jesus is no stained-glass figure, no pastel face on a religious card.*

Jesus was the incarnation of God, and yet in every way He was the most human of all human beings that has ever lived. He experienced without sin the same conditions that have plagued mankind since the beginning of time. Before Christ, there were laws no one could fulfill. The pathway to God was blocked by sin. But God couldn't bear the separation anxiety. Now, through His only Son's death, God offers us a gift of radical, undeserved, but completely available redemption.

There is now hope for all who claim His name. Jesus bridges the gap between humanity and God by becoming one of us. We are forever connected to Him in our humanity, so that the very painful experiences of our lives become our pathway to finding permanent residence in His strength.

ALTHOUGH JESUS LIVED A PERFECT LIFE, He knew what it was to experience extreme weariness and fatigue. Many times He left the people He was healing and set a limit on the number of miracles He performed. Many times He ceased teaching the great crowds. He retreated to rest because he was fully human and would become exhausted. Luke 4:42 tells us how Jesus "went to a lonely place," only to be tracked down by those who wanted more of Him. Jesus was not a celebrity who was always "on," or some Type-A person who made little room in His life for down time. He never apologized for needing time away for quiet and refreshment.

Jesus also experienced the messy emotion of anger. We read in Luke 19 how Jesus found that the temple had taken on the atmosphere of a flea market or busy mall. He called it "a hangout for thieves!" (as it's put in *The Message*'s paraphrase). Jesus was so angry He threw everyone out who had set up shop, and overturned the tables of the buyers and the sellers. He was righteous in His anger, and did what He knew was right before God.

He also became frustrated. In Luke 9 we read that His disciples were unable to drive a demon out of a boy. The boy's father pleaded with Jesus to have mercy on his child, and Jesus, in His frustration with His disciples, said, "What a generation! No sense of God! No focus to your lives! How many times do I have to go over these things? How much longer do I have to put up with this?" Then He told the man to bring his son to Him, and He healed him.

Jesus experienced the messiness of grief. He wept over His beloved city: "O Jerusalem, Jerusalem, how often I have longed to gather your children together, as a hen gathers her chicks under her wings, but you were not willing." Listen to the heart of Jesus—broken, distressed, and full of love and mercy!

He was rejected by many who heard Him, and in one instance was forced from the synagogue He'd been speaking at and run out of town! When He restored vision to a blind man on the Sabbath, He was accused of breaking the law. In John 5, we read how even His own brothers turned against Him.

Jesus lived one of the loneliest lives imaginable. As a single man who never married or had children, He must have experienced moments of longing for intimacy and companionship. His life was littered with disappointing friendships. Judas, one of His beloved disciples, betrayed Him with a kiss, which led to His death!

Jesus understands every tear you have cried over a lost love, over the betrayal of a best friend, over the heartbreak of having a deceitful business partner, over the pain of having an adulterous spouse, over the grief given you by children who spit in your face and walk away from the faith. Jesus knew the messiness of betrayal. He weeps with you! And through His resurrection, He tells us, "Don't give up! This isn't the end of the story! Let us weep together and move on into a new life!"

———

When God chose to send Himself into this world, He didn't put a buffer around His Son. The Father gave Him no easy way out. Jesus walked through many of the same messy moments we all do, in the company of messy people with messy lives.

And when He was on the eve of a terrible death by crucifixion, His agony was so intense that He sweat drops of blood. He knew He would become sin on the cross. He knew that God could not be in the presence of sin. And He knew that the worst, most grueling element of His sacrifice would be the absence of His Father in that hour. He wanted to avoid what lay before Him. But He also acknowledged the will of God.

Jesus went through the messiness of mockery and torture. After His betrayal by Judas and His arrest, Jesus was slapped by the palace guard, spit upon, and beaten. He was put through various trials that made a mockery of the law. He was whipped with a *flagrum,* which consisted of leather strands with metal and bone embedded in them. The Roman guards mocked Him—He was dressed in a robe, given a stick for a scepter, and then a heavy thorn crown, covering His entire scalp, was pressed down onto his head. After a sleepless night, Jesus was forced to walk more than two miles to the site of His crucifixion with a heavy crossbar—weighing well over 100 pounds—on His back.

Crucifixion is one of the most messy and cruel ways a human can die. Throw out the images of the calm, serene-faced Jesus hanging on a cross—the images we see in carvings, paintings, and stained glass windows. Jesus went through unspeakable torment for you and me on that cross. When it was laid on the ground, Jesus was placed on His back with His arms outstretched. Seven-inch spikes were driven into His wrists, through the median nerve, causing waves of pain to radiate through His body.

When the cross was placed upright, His shoulder and elbow joints became dislocated. His body was in a position that made breathing nearly impossible. At this point, He would have been suffering from acute dehydration, severe blood loss, and shock. He would have been expected to die of slow suffocation as fluid built up in His lungs and His heart gradually failed.

After hanging on the cross for nine excruciating hours, Jesus cried out, "My God, My God, why have You forsaken

Me?" In this cry, Jesus becomes fully human in His pain. It's every cry ever uttered from a human heart brutalized by the sin of the world. On the cross, a very human yet divine Jesus took upon Himself the agony of rejection, depression, despair, and hopelessness.

What other spiritual torments did He endure? Well, what better time for Satan to whisper defeat into His ears than when He hung naked on the cross? Imagine how He must have been taunted by the demons of hell. Jesus knew full well He could remove Himself from all this torment, but He chose to remain on the cross. This astounding love beyond love was His choice.

He could have put an end to the agony in the first hour.

But He chose to endure, to lay His life down.

What we should have suffered, He took upon Himself.

If you can embrace the mystery of Jesus as one who was human and also divine, your messy, human story will have meaning. No messy season of your life will put off a Savior who died such a messy, horrible death. You may turn to Him in the messiest times of your life.

But don't leave Him on the cross. Without Sunday— without His resurrection—we would have little to hope for. If there were no empty tomb, the human messiness of our lives would throw us, irrevocably, into the bottomless pit of defeat and despair. But because we serve a risen Lord, we too can now rise up and face the demands of a messy world, knowing that Jesus fully comprehends our condition.

> *God gave His Son to die,*
> *His heart broken,*
>> *so that we would never again be even a breath*
>> *away from His presence.*

Christ is risen,
    despite the messiness of our doubts,
    despite the darkness of our world.

We are forever accepted in all our messiness
    through the blood of Jesus Christ.
We cannot earn His love.
It is ours by grace.
And it's time for us to live like we are His children.

O blessed Christ!
Alleluia!
Now it all begins.

I ended my first book with the words, "No Answer." I know, Lord, why you utter no answer. You are yourself the answer. Before your face questions die away. What other answer would suffice?

C.S. LEWIS,
from *Till We Have Faces*

AFTERWORD

Since I began work on this book, life around here—life around the world—has gotten more messy than ever.

In the last six weeks, I've been to a funeral for a dear friend's six-month-old baby, and to a memorial service for another friend's 48-year-old wife, who died less than three months after being diagnosed with a rare blood cancer. I've seen two teen suicide attempts. One young, glorious man of God succeeded in robbing himself of the life God had for him to walk into. A glorious daughter of God misfired the weapon she had turned on herself, and her life, thankfully, still lies waiting before her.

Every day is a gift, a measure of manna from the hands of God. Every moment offers each of us the chance to reach out to a Jesus who knows how messy life is.

My prayers are that this book will, somewhere, beat back the darkness. I ask that some light might sear through into a life or heart that needs to feel, see, and believe that God does so love us all, that He inhabits our circumstances and meets us where we are—messy, tired, weary, doubting, hoping. Through Jesus, may the song of the destinies beyond our knowing sing on.

—Bonnie

NOTES

The Photos in God's Wallet

Page 9: "Our life is a short time…"
  Henri Nouwen, *The Wounded Healer* (New York: Doubleday, 1979).

Chapter 6—Living Water

Page 62: "Now we no longer believe…"
  John 4:42 AMP. Parentheses, brackets, and emphasis in original.

Chapter 9—God Heard

Page 88: "Don't I mean more…"
  1 Samuel 1:8.

Page 89: "I prayed for…"
  1 Samuel 1:27-28.

Chapter 10—Battling Fear, Remembering to Breathe

Page 94: "God did not give…"
  2 Timothy 1:7 AMP. Parentheses and brackets in original.

Page 97: "he and all the other…"
  Acts 10:2.

Page 103: "Come to Me…"
  Matthew 11:27-28 AMP. Parentheses, brackets, and emphasis in original.

Chapter 16—The Pharisee in Me

Page 156: "For our sake…"
  1 Corinthians 5:21 NRSV.

Chapter 18—Guess Who's Coming to Dinner?

Page 178: "Today is salvation day…"
  Luke 19:10 THE MESSAGE.

Chapter 23—Crossing the River

Page 214: "Love bears up…"
    1 Corinthians 13:7 AMP. Brackets and emphasis in original.

Epilogue—The Messy Life of Christ

Page 229: "hangout for thieves!"
    Luke 19:46 THE MESSAGE.

Page 229: "What a generation!"
    Luke 9:41 THE MESSAGE.

ACKNOWLEDGMENTS

It's impossible to imagine how this book would have come together—

...without the relentless encouragement of Terry Glaspey and Carolyn McCready at Harvest House. Shrines in their honor are in my immediate plans for our front yard.

...without the dinner with Bob Hawkins Jr. of Harvest House, where he wrote out the title of the book on our tablecloth and asked our server what she thought about "messy lives." I thank the entire staff of Harvest House for having the integrity of spirit and openness of heart to allow me to petition for a title like this.

...without the cheerleading section at my house—Brent, Courtney, and Graham—who put up with endless moaning and groaning from this reluctant yet eager author-in-the-making. My husband and children continue to be the backbone of my inspiration. I could not go on without their grace. I am not the cookie-baking mom or elegant southern housewife they deserve. They allow me to stumble through my attempts to speak hope to others—all done in the midst of their lives and mine, lived on a farm in Tennessee where there may some day be a clean kitchen and folded laundry.

...without the brilliant skill of an author/editor named Cindy Crosby, who took on putting together the pieces of this puzzle and crafting my passionate scribblings into a book. Because of her talents and skills, I've been allowed this chance to represent my view of a blindingly human and divine Jesus.

...without Scotty Smith, who continually inspires and threatens to flatten me with the challenges of his teaching, his speaking, his life, his honesty, his searching, his humble wrestling with the realities of Christ. He reads my mail, and then he sends me to the One who can answer it. Over and over again, I've heard Scotty use the "messy" word in his teaching. Perhaps that's where the germ of the book began years ago. Scotty was the first person to break through to my heart with the message of how vital it is to believe that God loves messy people.

…without the people who write to me, meet me at concerts, sign my prayer book, visit my Web site—who fall on me at times in tears, who find in my face a reflection of their own searching to know Jesus more…their searching for sanity, for purpose, for salvation in this upside-down world.

…without the generous input of Dr. David Teraska (www.AmericanBible.org), who helped me research the medical aspects of the death of God's Son by crucifixion.

…without the friendships of Lisa Bevill, Nan and Wayne Gurley, Jill Costello, Sue Buchanan, Mary Sue Curtis, Kerry and Phylis, Cheryl P., Cheryl R., Cheryl F.—my "C" posse women of faith—David A., Alan and Leah Scott, Merrill Ann, Russ and Tori, Debbie and Brian; and most importantly, the persistent loyalty and love of my immediate family: Mom and Dad, Amy and Stan.

…without the guidance and partnering energies of Malcolm Greenwood, Eric Darken and Bret Teagarden, Stormy Mitchell, Melissa Goodson, Tricia Ascherton, co-writers, Lowell Alexander, David Hamilton, Lisa Silver, and Suzanne Jennings.

…without all who allow me to be such a messy person and love me in spite of it. These men and women support my heart and soul, write songs and produce them, encourage me when I am ready to throw in the towel, arrange my travel—my ability to take the message of Jesus to others—and give me the bedrock gift of knowing, when I get out of bed each day, that I am part of a group of survivors in our ever-changing, never-changing profession of faith.

In the name of our precious Jesus, I thank every one of my forever friends and family, and I am especially indebted to the ones who were gracious enough to share their personal stories: Garry and Veronica, Parwin, Regina, Steve, Patty Sue, Marlei, Sue Bue, Mary George, Nanette, and Diana…May the Lord bless you for bearing witness by your stories that, because of the cross of Jesus, nothing is wasted.

With faith in our Christ, grace abounds for all of us in this ragtag world.

Soli Deo Gloria.

For information about recordings
of Bonnie Keen's music:

EB Music Group
www.ebmusicgroup.com
1-866-370-7431 (toll-free)

For information about scheduling Bonnie Keen
or to find out more about her ministry:

www.bonniekeen.com